The Slavic Community on Strike:
Immigrant Labor in Pennsylvania Anthracite

THE
SLAVIC COMMUNITY
ON STRIKE

Immigrant Labor in Pennsylvania
Anthracite

VICTOR R. GREENE

UNIVERSITY OF NOTRE DAME PRESS
NOTRE DAME   LONDON

To Laura,
who knows the work as well as I

*Winner of the
Kosciuszko Foundation
Doctoral Dissertation Award
for 1965*

Acknowledgments

Attempting to uncover motivation among inarticulate American nationalities is a difficult encounter indeed, and when the investigator is not a member of any one of them, the obstacles are even more formidable. Guidance and assistance are urgent necessities. I feel fortunate that I was well supplied with both and wish here to express my gratitude. The reader should know some of those who made it possible for me to uncover a little-known story of the American past. The events assumed a remarkably lifelike quality to the writer. Whether he conveys that impression and offers a convincing thesis is left to the judgment of the audience.

Essentially the work is a condensation of my doctoral dissertation written at the University of Pennsylvania, and readers who wish more extensive discussion and documentation are referred to it. I am grateful to Morton Keller, my supervisor, for saving me from major pitfalls, as well as to Thomas Cochran for his helpful suggestions. Mieczysław Giergelewicz and Ludwik Krzyzanowski at that time graciously advised a young graduate student in what can only be called the "Old World manner." Edward Pinkowski of Philadelphia was very generous with both his Polonia collection and knowledge.

The warmth of the people of anthracite made research in the fields a pleasure. Among the many I must designate Mrs. J. J. Kocyan and Joseph Tomascik of Wilkes-Barre; Matas Zujus of *Garsas;* Tom Barrett and Rev. J. Karalius of Shenandoah; Bishop Grochowski of the Polish National Catholic Church; Rev. W. Patkutka, Antanas Kucas, and Henry Dende of Scranton; and Daniel McGilvray, then Director of the Wyoming Historical and Geological Society. The Schuylkill County Historical Society was always helpful, as were the Pennsylvania Museum and Historical Commission in Harrisburg and the Hazleton Public Library.

At various stages of the work several colleagues kindly offered their invaluable criticisms and suggestions, as Philip Gleason of the University of Notre Dame, Timothy Smith of the University of Minnesota, and Carlton Qualey of Carleton College. Editorial help came from Mrs. Abigail Siddall and from John Ehmann of the University of Notre Dame Press. Eugene Kusielewicz of the Kosciuszko Foundation deserves particular mention for his association with the work.

Unfortunately the above recognizes only a small number to whom I am grateful. My greatest debt remains with the one to whom the work is dedicated, my wife.

MANHATTAN, KANSAS   VICTOR R. GREENE
JANUARY 30, 1968

Contents

Introduction

IN HUMAN TERMS THE DECLINE OF A ONCE-GREAT
industry is a tale of sadness. The anthracite coal fields of
eastern Pennsylvania no longer support the nearly three-
quarters of a million people that they did before World
War I, and mining communities are now hard put to
alleviate the current high unemployment and economic
distress. They are searching for a new commercial basis,
and gradually they are becoming successful. Still, the
business of mining is disappearing, and only the lucky
coal worker can find a job in his trade. Many families
must depend on work at a far distance or on the employment of wives and daughters.

Long-time residents compensate for the present gloom
by looking back and reminiscing about the flush days of
the black diamond. Such romantics describe the halcyon

era of the industry by recalling the magnificent coal-baron mansions along Wilkes-Barre's Fifth Avenue, South Franklin Street; the eccentric Packer House at Mauch Chunk; or the Pardee, Markle, and Coxe homes near Hazleton. Indeed, one is captivated by the epic nature of the industry as it was, the operation of hundreds of breakers and the army of hundreds of thousands responding to the call of the shrill mine whistles at dawn and dusk.

While one of the nation's major industries is in its last throes, the record of its very demise may have value to scholars. Two unique features of the anthracite area's recent past may attract the attention of American social historians: the wide ethnic diversity of the work force and the power of its union, the United Mine Workers of America. On the surface these two characteristics seem incompatible. In fact, an old and still widespread assumption holds that a multinational proletariat, especially one made up of the more recent immigrants of the second half of the nineteenth century, retarded labor organization.

To those natives affected by them the new immigrants were a puzzle. As some earlier nationalities had, they arrived here in response to industrialization; but originating from little-known lands in Eastern and Southern Europe, these masses appeared as a mystery. A good part of these newcomers, generally termed "Slavs," carried with them a cultural baggage, traditions, customs, and a family life with which this country was unfamiliar.[1] While many natives were uncertain as to what this new immigrant might mean to America, one group, labor leaders, received these arrivals coolly. The reason for their hostility was, they said, that Slavs confounded organization.

Yet, when one views the experience of unions in the anthracite fields in the nineteenth century, it becomes clear that if early labor organizers had investigated and sincerely attended to the Slavic community, they could have utilized its social structure to advantage. For far from weakening labor organization, the Polish, Lithuanian, Slovak, and Ukrainian mineworkers, their families, and their communities supported labor protest more enthusiastically than many other groups and were essential to the establishment of unionism permanently in the coal fields.

To be sure, the reader should not mistake the aim of this study. It does not claim that the incoming Slav was solely responsible for labor organization. The experience here does not offer proof of labor protest on an entirely ethnic basis. Some nonstrikers were new immigrants, and many union stalwarts were Anglo-American. In fact, the top-level union leadership was always non-Slavic. However, it was chiefly the East European anthracite society, and the United Mine Workers' eventual recognition of that group's militancy and cohesion, especially in times of crisis, which brought the union to the industry to stay.

In attempting to uncover the motivation of the Slavic nationalities in critical periods, the writer does not seek to explain forces affecting all the ethnic groups in the region. The newcomers as a whole acted more belligerently than earlier immigrants, but this study does not answer the question of why the rest of the rank and file appeared more passive. Such an analysis would have to be part of a complete social history of the anthracite fields, a task that is left to another writer. The issues dealt with here are the connection of the Slavic community with labor unrest, a possible explanation of that behavior, and the effect of the group's activities upon industrial relations before 1903.

In its external contact with industrial America the Slavic community appears, not as the demoralized, divided body that some have described, but as an unusually durable and rather determined society. On the other hand, the newcomers were not at all times a completely monolithic and unified aggregate. Ethnic, religious, and social differences were evident at various times. No new nationality escaped intra- or intergroup tensions. But certainly, during industrial stress at least, an East European identification appeared which temporarily submerged internal conflict and compelled union support.

The evidence drawn upon to demonstrate Slavic devotion to labor does not reveal any one particular institution as *the* motivating catalyst. Some of the most sensitive records for that kind of analysis, memoirs of local leaders, relevant parish documents, transcripts of fraternal branch meetings, and many local immigrant newspapers, are very likely lost forever. Most statistical and official documents proved unreliable in not designating nationality accurately. Recourse has been chiefly to the ethnic groups' own accounts, particularly parish histories, and the extant English and Slavic language newspapers.

I

The Locale

A VISITOR TO NORTHEASTERN PENNSYLVANIA TODAY IS AT
first favorably impressed by the beauty of the region.
Driving in summer from the Delaware River at the upper
corner of the state southwestward into Pike County and
through Wayne County, he encounters colorful natural
scenery and green, rolling countryside. But suddenly,
with an effect like that of a wrong note in a cadenza, the
gay landscape changes dramatically.

The metamorphosis is unpleasant. Just at Forest City
and on toward Carbondale, the reds, yellows, and greens,
formerly everywhere, begin to appear only in patches.
The more somber tones of brown, gray, and black dominate. The hills are now treeless, barren piles of coal
waste, debris scraped out from far underground. Any
slight wind blows fine coal dust from these culm dumps

1

into thin clouds, to obscure the view, and heavier smoke from burning underground mine fires contributes to the acrid haze. The countryside streams have long been sulfurous. Occasionally the remains of wooden buildings, abandoned breakers where coal was processed, raise their dark hulks against the sky. The pall of a dead industry introduces the visitor to the northern end of the Pennsylvania anthracite field.

But if the environment repels some travelers, it attracts others, for the concentrated locale of most of the world's anthracite reserves impresses the student of mineralogy. In America these coal beds can be found in Massachusetts, Rhode Island, Virginia, and the Southwest—Colorado, Arkansas, and New Mexico. But at the turn of the century Pennsylvania produced over 99 percent of the hard coal in the United States, which in fact was over three-quarters of the world production. The extent of the coal fields further emphasizes the compact nature of the industry. The area of workable hard coal in the late 1800's was just under five hundred square miles, less than half the size of Rhode Island, and was situated mainly in five counties: Lackawanna, Luzerne, Carbon, Schuylkill, and Northumberland. In all, the four geological sections of this hard-coal area measure only one hundred miles long and thirty miles wide. Popular writers and commentators commonly refer to a section in the region according to its trade division: the Wyoming, Lehigh, or Schuylkill field.

The Wyoming-Lackawanna, or northern, district is easily distinguished, as it is well separated from the others. Shaped in outline like a long canoe, it extends from Forest City in Susquehanna County fifty-five miles west to Shickshinny on the Susquehanna River. Its maximum width is just over six miles. Always the most populous of the three fields, the sector has two large cities, Wilkes-Barre and Scranton, which are the seats of Luzerne and Lackawanna counties respectively. Smaller communities situated above Scranton are Carbondale, Olyphant, Dunmore, and Dickson City (Priceburg). At the Luzerne, or western, end of the field, Pittston, Kingston, Plymouth, and Nanticoke complement Wilkes-Barre.

In addition to having the most inhabitants, Wyoming consistently outproduced the other two districts in hard coal in the late 1800's, to ship about half of the industry's total. Several factors accounted for the section's leadership. Operators found extraction to be easy, for the dip of the beds into the ground was gradual as it began at Forest City, reached maximum depth about Wilkes-Barre, and outcropped again at the western end. Thus its twenty beds lay in a horizontal pattern much like the bottom of a broad crescent. Broken faults were rare. Containing more carbon, the coal itself was much less impure here than elsewhere. In sum, then, the northern area mined the most and sent out the highest percentage of the marketable product.

Thirty miles south is the Lehigh, or middle, section, smallest of the three fields. It has an area of fifty-one square miles, one-fourth the size of the Wyoming district, and includes the eastern middle geological division centered about Hazleton and the southern basin to the east

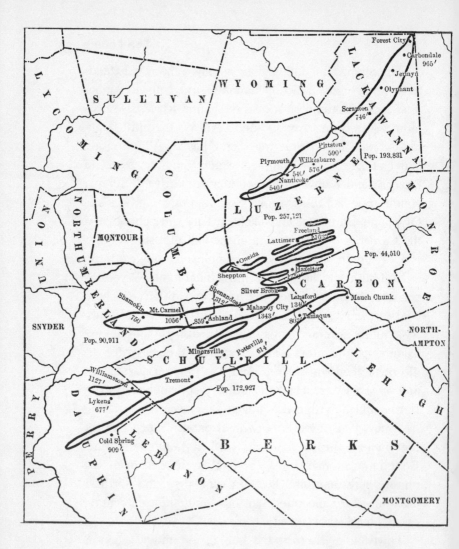

MAP OF PENNSYLVANIA ANTHRACITE AREA IN 1900

of Tamaqua. The Lehigh River roughly marks the eastern boundary of the middle field. On entering the basin from the north, the visitor encounters the so-called north side, the towns of Freeland, Drifton, Hollywood, and Lattimer. After going through Hazleton, he reaches the south side and the settlements of Audenried, Beaver Meadow, McAdoo, and Honey Brook. Off to the west stand two other hamlets known to every mineworker who was in the 1900 strike, Oneida and Sheppton.

Farther south over the mountain is the rest of the Lehigh basin. There nestled in the once-beautiful Panther Creek Valley are Tamaqua, Coaldale, Lansford, Summit Hill, and Nesquehoning, where the ugly scars of old mine shafts, abandoned railroads, and decaying structures now mar the natural beauty of the place.

The coal of the middle field lay in a bed over twenty-nine feet thick in strata steeper and more irregular than those in the northern basin and, thus, less accessible. The Lehigh region ranked last of the three fields in production, averaging about one-sixth the entire output before 1902.

The third of the trade regions is the largest in area— the Schuylkill field of 238 square miles. Actually the Schuylkill includes two geological divisions, the western middle sector reaching from near Carbon County to Columbia and Northumberland, and the southern basin west of Tamaqua almost entirely in Schuylkill County.

The communities here seem more quaint than others in the anthracite area. Shamokin, Mount Carmel, Mahanoy City, and especially Shenandoah bring to mind settlements in central Europe. Bulblike towers of Eastern churches and the crosses atop Catholic steeples dominate the mineworkers' homes clustered about the parish centers. Pottsville, however, the seat of Schuylkill County and its southernmost and largest city, has a more purely American character with a magnificent courthouse on a hill that dominates the vicinity.

While the largest field rated second of the three in coal production by turning out somewhat less than a third of the total, its reserves have always been the greatest, chiefly in the Mammoth Bed, a huge deposit famous for its size. The coal of this basin, however, was most impure, bony, and often mixed with sandstone. In addition miners found it least accessible because of sharply pitching veins at steep angles.

Treverton, at the western end of the Schuylkill district, completes a visitor's tour of the Pennsylvania anthracite area. The trip southward is unquestionably a depressing one. The transformation of timbered hills to nude piles of coal waste has destroyed any bucolic atmosphere. Once, years ago, before the coming of Western man, this area might well have looked like what one town (Mauch Chunk) now terms itself, "the Switzerland of America." But the arrival of an industry changed the natural complexion of the region.

While the industry must have depressed nature lovers when it appeared, it also was foreboding to unionists. The anthracite industry from its beginnings early in 1820 to its maturity about 1900 reflected the ordinary trend of American business, from competition to combination. By the turn of the century hard-coal production was a well-financed edifice of American capitalism, an industrial empire under the master financier J. Pierpont Morgan. After the anthracite area had experienced good times and bad, he fashioned a mighty trust which seemed able to withstand any attack, certainly one from any labor organization. Thus the establishment of a union in the field in 1903 stands as a truly phenomenal achievement.

Beginning after the War of 1812, the industry grew by stages. At first many budding entrepreneurs tried their hands at becoming coal barons. The shippers then were mainly canal companies, like the Delaware and Hudson (D and H) in Wyoming and the Lehigh Coal and Navigation (LC and N) in Lehigh. These two would become railroad operators later.

When the demand for coal mounted in the early 1860's, the old mining techniques proved insufficient, and greater investment was required. The marginal producers left the district, and larger mining companies appeared, to dig deeper mines and construct more expensive workings. The company that could afford ventilation fans, water pumps, and other technological advances replaced the single, pick-and-shovel capitalist.

Also a new shipper appeared, the railroad, to set the scene for the industry's next stage. The iron horse became a symbol of the mineowners' power, because as the railroads drove out their water-carrying competitors, they themselves began to unearth the black rock. All but one of the major roads, the Reading, had begun mining by the

7

end of the 1860's, in most cases through a subsidiary coal company. The producing-shipping leaders were the Lackawanna (Delaware, Lackawanna, and Western), the Pennsylvania, and the D and H in the north; Asa Packer's Lehigh Valley, the Central of New Jersey, and others in the middle district; and eventually, by the mid-1870's, the Reading in Schuylkill, the largest anthracite producer.

By the end of the 1870's, then, the coal industry assumed its mature financial structure, with the railroads in control. With the continued growth in demand and complexity of production, only these larger concentrations of wealth could maintain the deeper mines, the more skilled engineers, and the more complex machinery, like the breaker above ground where the coal was cleaned and sized.

A few independent mineowners hung onto their property and remained into the twentieth century. Located chiefly in the middle field, they were especially vigorous and very hostile to labor unions. These Lehigh mineowners well characterized the American ideal of rugged individualism. The earliest, Ario Pardee, began his company in 1840, and with a relative, Calvin, developed the Hazleton area deposits. The elder Pardee also helped another entrepreneur, George B. Markle, begin operations in 1858 and saw the latter prosper. After Markle's retirement in 1879, his son, John, a renowned mining engineer, continued to enlarge the business.[1] A third group, the Coxe Brothers, opened their mines at Drifton at the end of the Civil War. Eckley B. Coxe headed the enterprise in the late nineteenth century and as a mining

8

engineer became known for his work in coal-waste reclamation. But despite their tenacity, just as the canals had given way in the 1870's, the individual proprietor, too, was eventually eliminated.

The roads had practically destroyed competing transporters and independent producers. Now they thought they could dominate with ease this basic industry of a maturing nation. Yet the quarter-century after 1875 was no era of bliss for the anthracite owners. Having won the prize from others, they now fought among themselves for it. This internecine struggle presented an internal tug-of-war between those who wanted the profits of free competition and those who desired a modus vivendi to eliminate competition's evils. Time after time roads joined and agreed to limit shipments, but just as often suspicion and greed ended the cooperation. Various attempts at combination failed until near the turn of the century, when the anthracite carriers formed a more permanent industrial structure—a trust with J. P. Morgan and George F. Baer in control.

Market fluctuations and the evils of cutthroat competition always plagued the industry. Operators had tried to stabilize and control production even before the Civil War. In the southern area, for example, owners joined to set prices and combat labor unions in the late 1840's. Other Schuylkill operators attempted regulatory organizations in the next decade. And in the post-Civil War era overproduction and falling prices forced the mineowners to work toward closer cooperation.

The leading figure to bring order out of chaos in this

9

unstable market was the Reading road, especially its head in the 1870's, Franklin B. Gowen. Consistently when surpluses glutted the market, he and later Philadelphia and Reading presidents tried to effect durable pools. But the industrial combinations of 1873, 1878, 1880, and 1884 repeatedly failed when a major producer objected to the allotted production or shipping percentages. J. P. Morgan tried his hand at solving the industry's woes in 1886, when, after conferring with all the railroad presidents, he made another pact. But this one, too, failed within two years.[2]

After the Reading went bankrupt in 1893 in trying to monopolize all production by land purchasing, Morgan decided to take a firmer grip. He created the so-called railroad "community of interest," an arrangement which was to bring stability lasting to World War I. In 1896 he allotted new quotas, and after reorganizing the Reading in 1897, he placed its president, George F. Baer, at the head of the trust. Another firm, the Temple Iron Company, provided the instrument for consultation, agreement, and enforcement. The ultimate degree of combination was at hand to control effectively the major producers.

Achieving stability through monopoly had encountered external obstacles as well as internal ones. These delays originated either from the public—for example, the periodic investigations by the New York, New Jersey, and Pennsylvania legislatures—or from the independent operators of the middle region. The latter objected to the shippers' discrimination and even intended to build their own rail carrier. But Morgan, Baer, and the Temple Company easily avoided any state regulation and forced the dissident independents to surrender their line.

By 1900, then, Baer and Morgan could look at the industry's growth with great satisfaction. The railroads had replaced the canals, and then, receptive to new techniques, had gone on to solve their most difficult problem, disciplining the trade. The recent, fitful cycle of agreement, sabotage, and devastating freedom for carrier-operators had come to an end. For the Morgan Community now securely enlisted the major carrier-producers: the Reading, Central of New Jersey, Erie, Lehigh Valley, Lackawanna, Delaware and Hudson, and Pennsylvania. Recurrent objections by the public seemed ineffectual, and the recent protests from independents were stilled. The new century began with an unparalleled era of trade peace, a peace that financiers believed no one could disturb, not even unionists in their attempts at labor organization.

The men of capital had struggled to bring stability to the industry and certainly were not willing to tolerate interference in their business from any labor union. Yet their grand edifice was not to withstand the introduction of a new proletariat into their work force, the East European American. This demographic change in the anthracite population had been going on while Morgan and others had been effecting the industrial combination. The new technology and greater output demanded an army of unskilled workers, and the first arrivals in the area, the skilled English and Welsh miners, had already been sup-

11

plemented by less-skilled Irish immigrants before 1870. But now all three watched a new element, the Slav, enter the work force, and they wondered whether he would raise or debase their own position. The operators welcomed the newcomers as additional manpower and hoped that their coming would prevent unionization. As events would show, this expectation was not to be fulfilled.

Thus both mineowner and Anglo-Saxon mineworker pondered the effects of the stranger. Few people had any idea of the immigrant's motivation. He came across the ocean with strange customs from a little-known region. Why had he left home? What did he want when he entered the anthracite mining communities?

II

From Old World to New

FOR SOCIOLOGISTS AND HISTORIANS TO DISCOVER MOTI-vating forces in the Slavic migrations of the late 1800's is not an easy task. Social scientists would naturally welcome survey results, but such data are not always available. And to complicate the problem, indirect techniques must be used to examine an inarticulate subject like the pre-1900 Polish immigrant. The only intimate documents are letters sent between the Old World and the New, and these, too, are somewhat scarce. Few such records exist for the period before the turn of the century.[1]

But other materials and approaches can lead to conclusions about motivation. Census and immigration statistics, though necessarily incomplete, especially before the twentieth century, can describe something about the newcomers. Figures show the time of arrival and other vital traits like age, skills, education, marital status, and so forth. And a review of living conditions abroad would uncover some of the major propelling forces. This information along with a brief sketch of the crossing itself will surprise those who regard these groups as ignorant, pliable, frightened souls in a state of shock and thus easily influenced by agents and harpies. To the contrary, the newcomers were on the whole intelligent, and they well knew why they were leaving and where they were headed.

Most appeared in America in the steamship age. Few Slavs arrived before 1880. By 1860, Italy, Russia, and Austria-Hungary together were the source of less than 1 percent of the entrants into America (1,076), and in the next decade the percentage was just about the same.[2] The decided shift came in the 1880's. While 52 percent arrived in that decade from northern and western Europe, 16 percent came from southern and eastern Europe. And thereafter the latter group continued its disproportionate increase. Just after the turn of the century the Anglo-Saxons constituted about 14 percent (137,900 out of 937,400), and the Slavs, over 60 percent (614,500). The 1900's as a whole showed the same proportion, about 12 to 65.[3]

At the end of the nineteenth century industrial America was attracting people from distant parts of Europe, and as the total number of these newcomers grew, the ethnic types proliferated. The many nationalities situated between the two largest peoples of east-central Europe, the Germans and the Russians, helped make the United

14

States even more heterogeneous than it was. Lithuanians, Poles, Czechs, Slovaks, Ruthenians and Ukranians, Magyars, Rumanians, Serbs, Croats, Slovenes, Bulgarians, Macedonians, and others added their contribution to American life. Two of these nationalities together, the Poles and the Lithuanians, made up the largest percentage of the East Europeans coming over. A closer study of their immigration figures will show where they came from, and when, why, and how they came.[4]

Polish aliens entered in ever-increasing numbers after 1870. The yearly average of Polish immigrants from 1870 to 1910 shows a gradual rise in the first two decades of the period from an annual average of 18,000 during the 1870's, through a dip in the 1890's, to a sharp rise to almost 100,000 in the early 1900's. During these years three empires occupied what had been Poland: Russia, Austria-Hungary, and Germany after 1871. Immigration records prove that the call of America spread over these lands from west to east.

Until 1890 it clearly was Prussia which sent most (three-quarters) of the Polish immigrants bound for the United States.[5] Apparently early German emigrants relayed home the news of the paradise, and the western Poles, knowing the language, communicated the information quickly throughout their own group.

The Poles of the two other areas, in Russia and Austria-Hungary, more than replaced their brothers to the west in the movement to America. Those from Galicia under the Hapsburgs, and Congress Poland under the Romanovs, began their international movement at about the time that the German Polish exodus declined. Though the group from the tsardom started late, it was to be the largest of the three Polish elements in the United States by 1900, a predominance it would never relinquish. The 1900 census records that of the total foreign-born Poles in America, who numbered over a third of a million, 39 percent came from Germany, 40 percent came from Russia, and 15 percent came from Austria-Hungary.[6] In the six years between 1899 and 1904 the entrants from the western sector made up only 5 percent of the total Polish immigration, while those from Austria-Hungary and Russia contributed the other 46 and 49 percent. Meanwhile, the Poles' northeasterly neighbors, the Lithuanians, heard of and joined the exodus. The numbers of incoming Lithuanians more than doubled between 1899 and 1903, from 6,858 to 14,432.

Polish settlement in the Pennsylvania anthracite region shows the same regional succession as is found in the overall immigration pattern, with German Poles coming first and Russian Poles later. In 1900 Russian Poles made up 64 percent of the nationality in the area, and German Poles, 11 percent.[7]

The continually eastward spread of the migration fever suggests that coercion by steamship or labor recruiters was less influential in stimulating emigrants than normal word-of-mouth communication. If agents had been the compelling force for movement, the emigration sources would have been more random than contiguous. The finding suggests, then, that the exodus stemmed from some local situation rather than from external persuasion.

Further attributes of the typical immigrant, although in some cases uncertain because of the absence of complete surveys in the early years, can be implied from immigration data. The earliest Polish arrivals, those from the Eastern Marches, arrived with their families; they were somewhat older than their immigrant countrymen to the east and were probably better educated. Official American records give more specific information on the later Polish and Lithuanian immigrants for the five-year period before 1904. Males counted for almost three-quarters of the total; almost all were between fourteen and forty-five years of age. More significant was the surprisingly high literacy rate; 71 percent of the Poles and 64 percent of the Lithuanians could read and write. For the period 1899 to 1909 the Polish literacy rate was eleventh of thirty immigrant nationalities.[8]

A final characteristic is perhaps the most helpful for an understanding of the Pole's life in the Old World—his trade. A few of those who were asked did not answer the question of occupation, and many more who did were women and children with no job at all. But of those who replied, more than eight of every ten of the Lithuanians and Poles were either farmworkers or simply manual laborers of some other sort. In other words, a decided majority were unskilled.[9] The conclusion is clear. Most were peasants with an agrarian background.

Statistics, then, tell a great deal about the typical Polish or Lithuanian immigrant as he disembarked at New York harbor sometime before 1903. Almost definitely he sailed to America after 1870; more exactly, sometime during the 1880's or about the turn of the century. If the Pole sailed before 1890, most likely his home was in the German provinces; if after that date, when many Poles did head for Pennsylvania, he probably left the Russian or Austro-Hungarian empire. Most likely he made the trip without female companionship; perhaps he had not yet taken a wife, but little real proof of his marital status exists for this period. He was probably in the full bloom of manhood, as the records of the time counted few children or old people, and well able to withstand the hardships of the voyage. While not well educated, he could read and write in his own language. But, above all, the average Polish or Lithuanian immigrant was a peasant, a man of the soil, who knew best how to grow crops and raise animals. His experience with urban and industrial areas was limited, although according to recent theories he was probably better able to handle his affairs, including a new work situation, than those whom he left behind.[10]

But figures do not illuminate another, more significant, aspect of immigration. They do not tell why, so tied to the soil, the migrants would leave their native lands and journey over four thousand miles to a strange environment. What were they looking for in America? The answer is undoubtedly economic advancement, a pursuit of wealth which would influence the newcomer's attitude toward employment. To understand the motives of Pennsylvania-bound Slavs, one must return to the Old World and take note of the political and economic conditions that forced them to leave.

Nineteenth-century political history is not a happy one in the memory of Polish and Lithuanian nationalists. In 1795 Prussia, Austria-Hungary, and Russia partitioned Poland for the third time in twenty-three years, and the subject people would not rewin independence for over a century. Russia held the largest section: Congress Poland and Lithuania. The Germans received the western third, the Eastern Marches, while Austria-Hungary took the smallest section, generally termed Galicia. As the century progressed, sporadic attempts at revolution followed by suppression occurred, but the peasants, the agricultural masses, largely ignored politics. Their concern was for their daily bread, and for that reason they would move to America.

A nearly medieval tradition of lord and serf prevailed in the German sector, as in the others, throughout the nineteenth century, with only very gradual emancipation. The Polish peasants of the Eastern Marches ignored the revolutionary currents of the 1830's and 1840's and took no part in them. They suffered generally from bad harvests in the late forties and middle fifties, and a general decline in prices.

Meanwhile German policy proved detrimental to the substantial Poles of the agricultural class. The Hohenzollerns had been freeing the serfs in Germany, and incoming Germans bought estates in Poland and dispossessed their eastern neighbors.[11] In addition the *szlachta*, the Polish landed gentry, lost much in the abortive mid-century revolution, and, heavily in debt, they sold more than a million acres to the Germans in the next forty

19

years.[12] The Prussian government financially encouraged the land transfer, and a movement of peoples began. The German landlords increasingly attracted the poorer Polish farmworkers from Russia and Galicia, while the Prussian Poles moved on to the more industrialized areas of Western Europe and the United States. The Polish mass migration was under way.

Certainly religious persecution was no cause for the Polish exodus. True, Bismarck did attack the Catholic Church in his Kulturkampf about 1874, and he began to arrest and replace the Polish clergy. And the Chancellor de-Polonized the provinces in other ways, for example, by secularizing education and banning the use of the Polish language, all of which did send some Polish clergy elsewhere, even to the United States. But the policy had less of an effect on the peasant bound for America. During the anti-Catholic attack in the 1870's more Poles moved to western Germany than to the United States, and the religious persecution ended about 1880, before the huge migration of Prussian Poles to America began.

A later chancellor, Von Bulow, also launched an anti-Polish campaign between 1898 to 1908. But its effect on migration was minimal. Polish resistance stiffened, and the emigration rate in that period fell sharply. Another often-designated motivation, avoidance of military conscription, may have encouraged some Polish youths to flee. However, an American consular official in Pomerania reported that the draft there was only a minor factor in the outward movement.[13]

Government policy, then, in Prussian Poland probably

had little influence on the outgoing Polish peasant. In Galicia the Austro-Hungarian government officially treated Poles well, but economic conditions made life difficult. The dominant enterprise, agriculture, had to support eight out of every ten inhabitants. Yet, with soil productivity poor and the growing season very short, misery was widespread. Industrialization might have helped the peasant, but down to 1908 Polish landlords themselves effectively stifled economic change in fear of the consequences.

As far as politics were concerned, the Hapsburgs maintained an enlightened rule over the Poles. The Emperor had freed the serfs in 1848, and he appointed a Polish provincial governor who instituted many salutary political reforms, including better ethnic representation. In 1869 the Empire allowed a local parliament to function and send delegates to Vienna, and by 1890 even the masses had a spokesman when Wicenty Witos was able to enter politics with his Peasant (later Popular) party.

So here, as in Prussian Poland, no political oppression forced out the peasant, simply because there was none. In the so-called Golden Age of Galicia in the half-century before 1914 existed the paradox of increasingly lenient political rule but ever-growing numbers leaving. Certainly Poles in Austria-Hungary had other than political reasons for their departure.

Material considerations were uppermost among the Russian Polish peasants also. Russia had won the lion's share of Poland in 1795, and so as many Poles lived there in the 1800's as in either of the other regions. As

21

in Galicia and Prussian Poland, as late as 1897 over three-quarters of the population lived in rural areas. Tsar Alexander II copied his Hapsburg counterpart and relieved the serfs of their feudal dues in 1864 in a political move to win Lithuanian and Polish peasant support following the abortive revolt in 1863. The ruler continued favoring the lower Polish classes at the expense of the upper by expropriating the property of many of the nobles. The agrarian masses received more largess in 1864 in the form of the *gmina,* which, like the Russian *mir,* allowed for some local self-government.

There was religious persecution, evident first about 1870, but it affected the peasant little. Russification of the Catholic Church weakened markedly by the end of the century when Russian Polish emigration swelled. The Tsar even permitted religious toleration about 1905, but the exodus continued to augment. So if it was effective at all, religious policy influenced emigration decisions probably only in the years before 1900.

Military service, too, counted as a minor factor, since it had been in effect at least a decade before the exodus began, and other indications point away from a general conscription and harsh Russian suppression. For the ten years after 1893 emigration rates were far from uniform within Polish Russia; some agrarian provinces in the Congress sent out many times more migrants than others. And, finally, many Poles as well as Lithuanians began moving into the teeth of the Russian bear as early as the 1880's. Having served in the tsarist army in the Empire proper and noted better living conditions, the oppressed groups were forming large colonies in the Moscow and St. Petersburg industrial areas.[14] Polish peasants would hardly be escaping from military service or religious persecution by living closer to the Tsar.

Thus, official government policy of the three Polish masters does not seem to explain the motives of emigrants leaving their land. The agrarian masses paid little attention to politics in Vienna, Berlin, and St. Petersburg. Communication beyond the province, and even more so beyond national boundaries, had been rare. The little village had been the peasant's world for centuries. Each member of the family, just as each family in the self-sufficient community, performed his role in a confined area. But now new influences, largely economic, altered these relationships and drove the Polish agrarian from his ancestral home. Economic conditions in the villages were growing worse for two major reasons: the first was an inefficient land system unable to support the second, a booming population.

A village in any of the three Polish sectors in the early 1890's, with its quiet road past simple cottages, might have at first looked idyllic in its rustic setting. The blue sky, the brown thatch, and the whitewashed walls of the gaily decorated huts would perhaps bring to mind romantic tales of noblemen and their trusty villeins. But on closer inspection one feature would strike one forcibly —the poverty. From any standard the peasant's material circumstances were poor and chronically so.

All peasant habitations in Poland were much the

same: small huts grouped along a dirt road and surrounded by mud, filth, and a few stray dogs, some chickens, and perhaps a duck. The interior confirmed the exterior destitution. A hall separated two dark rooms, living quarters on the left and a combined tool shed and barn on the right.

The living area was dominated by a large brick stove, which served for cooking as well as for a bed for the family in cold weather. Straw mats covered part of the earthen floor. A bench stood at one side, and the only other furniture was a table and a chest. A crucifix hanging over the doorway and perhaps a gilded picture of the Virgin above the chest provided the only interior decoration. The Slavic peasantry wore inadequate clothing. The men, with large handlebar mustaches, wore no hats, but the women wore kerchiefs. When working in the fields, the women used their skirts and wide aprons as sacks. Most villagers had no footwear, although a few distinguished males wore high boots into which they stuffed their cotton trousers.

The village provided the peasant a rather fixed setting, one in which the family and its role in an agricultural community were valued far more than the individual.[15] The major interests of such a community were two: the religious and spiritual life of its members, who observed Roman Catholic ritual particularly concerning Mariology and veneration of the saints, and their attachment to the soil for material and even mystical satisfaction.

The immediate problem in life was of course earning a living, and peasant society, with the family as the productive unit, provided the means and the environment. The family subordinated private affairs, births, marriages, and deaths to its will. All members by their joint labors had to contribute to maintaining or hopefully raising the family's position in society: only by working the land could the masses hope to advance. The free peasants sought to become rich peasants; the rich peasants, the equivalent of lesser nobles; and so on.

The Polish masses, however, encountered increasingly difficult agricultural conditions for a variety of reasons. One was an uneconomic distribution of land, especially in Russia and Austria-Hungary. The parceling of land retarded productivity. In addition, superstition, customs, and traditional practices wasted the already niggardly soil.

The great population increase intensified an already serious food shortage. As a devout Catholic, the Slav never thought of limiting his family. The prolific Pole in the 1890's had a birth rate one-sixth above the European average (43.5 per 1,000), and by World War I it was the highest on the continent.[16] The fertility of the Polish woman even troubled her European masters. According to Chancellors Bismarck and Von Bulow the "rabbitlike" increase of the subject nationality sabotaged the German colonization campaign in the heavily Polish Eastern Marches, and the other two areas watched the multiplying Poles with equal dismay. Even while the Polish exodus was drawing off some of the surplus, the population of Congress Poland from 1860 to 1900 nevertheless increased by 180 percent, while the Galician

25

population grew by 80 percent.[17] In sum, then, the estimated total inhabitants in what was to be modern Poland doubled in the last half of the nineteenth century to about 25 million.[18] It is no wonder, then, that about 1900, fifty thousand people starved every year in Galicia, and Russian Poland had annually to import millions of dollars' worth of foreign grain.[19]

It was the psychological torment of sinking to a landless state that was especially unbearable for the peasant. He was particularly unwilling to surrender his position as a propertied farmer. The land to him was more than that from which he drew his sustenance. His whole world, his customs, superstitions, indeed his entire being, revolved about the good earth. And the village associated the family's social position with landholding. So while conditions worsened, the plowman held onto his plot as long as possible and tried to eke out an existence for his wife and children. For to lose land, even a part of it, was to lose dignity.[20] Often, therefore, to avoid such a loss the choice was made to enter the labor market and the commercial world in order to purchase that which gave life meaning, sufficient land. The result was the formation of a peasant proletariat roaming the countryside, indeed the world, for employment in agriculture and industry.

Most Prussian Poles, other than those in already industrialized Silesia, headed for western Germany. In Congress Poland, where more than 1 million agriculturalists were looking for work in the late 1880's, growing industrialization was helping to solve the problem. With German assistance the Tsar turned Poland into the workshop of the Empire, and Russia was employing six times as many workers in heavy industry in 1900 as it had in all industry in 1850.[21]

In Galicia industrialization did not absorb the peasant surplus because the economy never had matured. The poor had to emigrate, to cross national boundaries, at least temporarily.

Some Poles, probably most, stayed on the continent, but others yielded to the lure of the New World, particularly Pennsylvania. Wage comparisons alone would attract them. Russian unskilled workers in the twenty-five years before 1900 received at most thirty cents a day, one-fourth the wage ($1.15) of their counterparts in American anthracite labor; the pay in 1891 for unskilled laborers in Austro-Hungarian Poland (twenty-four cents) was about one-fifth that in the United States; and farm and factory labor in Poznania East Prussia got one-half (sixty cents) the American average for the unskilled worker in the 1880 to 1900 period.[22]

Such comparisons are not academic, since many simple peasants did have these facts. Knowledge of American opportunities, even of pay scales, was accessible to Polish villagers. The information came through the mail in the form of the immigrant letter. Correspondence back home from earlier Slavic emigrants was not just a letter home but indeed a social obligation. Although it demanded a sacrifice of time and a tedious, reflective effort on their part, immigrants considered letter writing a duty to old-country relatives. Distance stretched family bonds but at

27

first did not break them. Polish villagers regarded mail and the information therein as communal, not individual, property, and when the letter arrived, with the usual enclosed photograph, it was passed quickly from hand to hand through the village.

Two authorities on the United States Immigration Commission of 1907 singled out the effect of the letter on Slavic migration: "In the large majority of cases . . . the immediate inducement to emigrants to leave home and sail for America comes in the form of personal letters from friends or members of their own families already in the United States."[23] The letter gave the anxious European agrarian the most effective and reliable description of wages and conditions in America.

The influence of a final incentive, the propaganda of transportation companies and labor agents, is conjectural. Some contemporaries accused these agents of exploiting the poor, ignorant peasantry and forcing them to leave the security of home. The outlandish exaggerations and promises circulating among the peasants were condemned. But propaganda itself could not have been the sole or major stimulant. If the peasant rooted in his land had been reasonably happy with his traditional environment, no amount of cajoling could have forced him to move. Thus the influence of these persuaders must not have been basic.[24] Whether from German, Austro-Hungarian, or Russian Poland, the immigrant left chiefly for economic reasons, to make money—"za chlebem."[25]

So the peasant never really sensed political oppression and hardly felt the pressure of the noneconomic causes.

The agreement among writers concerning motive is striking:

> Religious and political motives have sunk into insignificance. . . . (With the exception of the Jews) . . . the main cause of immigration at the present time [is] economic. . . .
>
> The present movement of population from Europe to the United States is, with few exceptions, almost entirely . . . economic. . . . Even in countries where [other political and religious] incentives prevail the more important cause is economic. . . .
>
> In general, economic rather than political conditions motivated the greatly increased [Polish] immigration to America after 1880. . . .
>
> The struggle for an existence drove us to America; With low wages in agriculture, with industry unable to absorb the surplus population, . . . emigration was a necessity for the agricultural laborer or landed peasant. . . .
>
> The pressure of economic necessity . . . too great for him to bear it any longer, [the Pole] had to go in search of better working and living conditions; Economic motives almost exclusively predominate in the emigration of [Polish] peasants . . . .

and finally,

> Masa glowna a przybyla do tej ziema-za chłebem, niewielki tylko odsetek przypada na inne przyczyny opuszenia Ojczyny (Most came to this country—for bread, only a small percentage left the old country for other reasons).[26]

The factors stimulating Lithuanian migration were

similar according to sources, especially the floods and droughts of 1867 and 1868. More than likely Lithuanians in or near Congress Poland experienced the same conditions as the Poles there.

Thus, it was the desire for wealth which forced the Slav to America. But one must avoid the further conclusion that the immigrant was what restrictionists labeled "the garbage of Europe." Those leaving the Old World certainly were not destitute. Besides the relatively high degree of literacy, Slavic immigrants brought above-average wealth. Many actually owned land or their families did (though not enough), and some at least must have been able to pay the costs of making the journey. Thus sheer grinding poverty did not force emigration, especially abroad. The real cause was probably the hope of acquiring income to reestablish the peasant in his old position in the village. He intended his migration to be temporary, just long enough to win American money to restore his status as a self-sufficient old-country landowner: "Le paysan avide de terre, attaché passionement a la glèbe, lui fait tous les sacrifices possible. Il va chercher de l'argent en Amérique dans le labeur écrasant des mines et des usines."[27] To Balch this attempt to regain or improve his position was "the sting which induces [a Pole] to fare overseas or to send out his son to the new land from which men come back with savings."[28] The sociologists Thomas and Znaniecki agreed: "When a peasant emigrates, it is usually with the desire to earn ready money and return home and buy land," for "the emigrant to America means to return a different man, to obtain—by earning much and spending little—the economic foundation on which to build a new superior career."[29]

The crossing itself, it has been suggested, also seriously disoriented the newcomer to America by causing considerable material and psychological distress. Indeed, it might well appear that a peasant people would suffer from a long sea voyage. However, while this new experience may have unnerved some, romantics could easily overdraw the passage. Several important factors mitigated the distress.

For example, government restrictions had little effect upon anyone determined on moving. European regulations to the turn of the century were almost nonexistent and, even where elaborate, as in Russia, were violated with impunity.[30] The significance of laws in America was equally as superficial; rejected migrants were always a small percentage.[31] The cost of the passage was no obstacle and hardly impoverished the traveler. A ticket from Europe to Wilkes-Barre in this period was twenty-six dollars, and lower during frequent rate wars.

The conditions aboard ship were of course not luxurious or even comfortable, but they also were not intolerable. Most of the steerage Poles and Lithuanians went in good company. The early arrivals in the 1880's normally brought a part of their family, and even later-coming bachelors and dependents accompanied relatives or friends. The most prevalent malady was seasickness according to one source, but this discomfort did not prevent the existence of social amenities which made the voyage almost a pleasure.[32]

The observers also may have exaggerated the exploitation of immigrants at receiving stations. If the arrival did not have the means to continue his journey beyond Castle Garden or Ellis Island, correspondents were available even in the form of national welfare agencies. One Polish organization, St. Joseph's Society, at the turn of the century was offering annually free lodging to four thousand newly arrived immigrants.[33]

Thus, when the Slavic newcomer to the Pennsylvania anthracite area came with one overpowering aim—to save money for his sought-after Old World parcel, he probably was not the naive rustic often pictured by filiopietists or sympathetic social workers. More likely the immigrant was a man with a definite purpose for coming, with knowledge, some intelligence, and a determination to succeed. As the future would show, he would challenge any obstacle, even the combination of anthracite operators, to realize his goal.

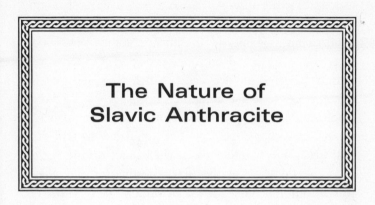

The Nature of Slavic Anthracite

A STRANGER IN THE PENNSYLVANIA ANTHRACITE AREA
after 1875 could easily recognize an East European immigrant society. The nucleus of the Slavic community was
the cherished institution that the migrant had brought
with him, his beloved parish.

While individual immigrants may have lived in the
small mining towns for some time, it was only with the
formation of a parish that an active community came into
existence. The Roman Catholic parish offered a common
social medium; in fact, the words "settlement" and "parish" in Polish, Lithuanian, and Slovak are identical. This,
however, means, not that the church or priest dictated
community life, but only that an inhabitant used the religious designation as a frame of reference and the parish
as a source of East European connections, a base of

operations which could be called upon during work disputes. Most parishes started as multinational Slavic colonies. In time the different ethnic groups usually separated, to form more homogeneous units but to maintain close relationships. Many small Slavic colonies never fragmented but remained harmoniously diverse.

In the setting of the parish, which gave substance to the Slavic American community, how successfully did the laborer pursue his quest for wealth? His strong drive for income and savings continued to influence his life in the coal fields and would have a vital effect during strikes.

A general view of the Slavs' destination indicates a concentration around the factory smokestack. Slavic settlements became really synonymous with the rising heavy industries such as steel, coal, and meat packing. It is no wonder so many found the Commonwealth of Pennsylvania attractive in the late nineteenth century. In the decade after 1890 more Polish parishes were constructed in the old Quaker haven than in any other state, and Lithuanians accompanied their Old World neighbors in number. One estimate counted fifteen thousand Lithuanians there in 1885 and two hundred thousand by 1915.[1]

The anthracite area especially came to look more and more like East Europe. The growth of the Slavic element coincided with the exit of the old English, Welsh, Irish, and strictly German nationalities. Whereas the English-speaking groups in the hard-coal region made up 94 percent of the foreign-born in 1880, the figure dropped to less than 52 percent twenty years later. The Slavic races meanwhile had grown from about 2 percent to over 40 percent, and the Poles, constituting the largest of the Slavic nationalities, multiplied eighteen times, to thirty-eight thousand.[2] In 1896 the largest company in the industry, the Philadelphia and Reading Coal and Iron Company, employed more Polish-born workers than any other group, including native Americans. In a random sampling of two-fifths of all anthracite mineworkers in 1903, Poles ranked second to the native Americans.[3]

At the beginning Poles and Lithuanians were indistinguishable, and they were joined by a few stray Ukrainians and Slovaks. Even though in many cases nationalism later gave birth to separate ethnic parishes, all Slavs made up one community in the Anglo-American world. At least to 1903 they came from a similar background, for the same job, for the same purpose; Slavdom was a definable social entity in eastern Pennsylvania long before the turn of the century.[4]

Poles and Lithuanians together first entered at the western edge of the southern field. Authorities fix the establishment of the first Polish-Lithuanian settlement in 1870 at Shamokin, with the organization of St. Stanislaus Roman Catholic parish. The two groups separated, however, shortly after a new wave of Lithuanian immigration in 1885; St. Michael's Lithuanian parish was created in 1892.[5] Above all others, the town of Shenandoah stands as the most multinational of any in the anthracite region, the model "melting pot" as it were. This locality, perhaps a test case in the Slavs' interrelations, was to become a center of immigrant labor activity. In the one-square-mile town, established groupings of English, Irish, Welsh, and Germans lived in close proximity to the Polish, Lithuanian, Ukrainian, and Slovak colonies. This Slav-Anglo-Saxon familiarity led to more than contempt; it was to make for labor riots.

The intermixture of Lithuanians and Poles in Shenandoah clouds the purely ethnic beginnings of East European settlement.[6] Both nationalities claim community founders of their own, but the bilingual Father Andrew Strupinskas (the Poles call him Strupinski) satisfied both sides. Authorities registered the new St. Casimir's parish in 1874 as Polish. The parish grew quickly and absorbed the increasing Slovak and Ruthenian (western Ukrainian) immigrants, who passed under the Polish wing, to receive assistance in settlement and job-hunting.[7]

But the intimacy grew stifling and secessions began. Ethnic self-consciousness arose to cause the Ukrainians to object to the Polish priest Father Joseph A. Lenarkiewicz, who, they felt, was suppressing their national character. Eventually they went to the town's leading East European, the Lithuanian Carl Rice, to help them bring over their own religious leader, Rev. John Wolansky.[8] This pioneer then went on to establish several Ukrainian parishes throughout the anthracite area. Meanwhile, after a legal suit over title to St. Casimir's, the Lithuanians in Shenandoah established their own place of worship in 1891, and the Poles spawned a new church, the Russian Polish St. Stanislaus, in 1898.[9] This church at times assumed a dual national character, for both Polish and Lithuanian priests served in its early years.

Thus the interconnection of all East Europeans seems to have characterized Shenandoah's early days. All joined the same church at the start, and Poles and Lithuanians assisted Ukrainians as well as each other. When a split did occur along ethnic lines, ties were not broken completely, as the Ukrainian dependence upon a Lithuanian and Lithuanian priests in Polish parishes show.

The Slavs in Mt. Carmel, another nearby mining town, underwent a similar experience. Lithuanians and Poles were indistinguishable ethnically at the start, and a Shamokin Polish priest aided the founding of this third East European parish, St. Joseph's, in 1877. In 1892 some Lithuanians and Slovaks went their own way, and four years later Russian Poles started their own church. One source specifically noted frequent Polish-Lithuanian intermarriage up to and probably after the 1890's.[10]

The other new major immigrant community, Mahanoy City, lay just to the east of Shenandoah. Here about 1888 a Lithuanian priest assisted his nationality and probably a handful of Poles to start their own church, but apparently friction developed. Five years later the Poles bought an old Baptist structure in which to perform their own religious ceremonies. After 1895 the nearby Minersville Poles went to the Lithuanian church, where every other Sunday the sermon was in Polish.[11] Other nearby Polish and Lithuanian settlements developed according to similar patterns.

The 1890 and 1900 census figures for Polish-born inhabitants in the anthracite area reveal a boom and a marked shift in settlement to the north, reflecting the later

Austro-Russian wave that deflected more Poles to the upper two counties, Luzerne (Wilkes-Barre-Hazleton) and Lackawanna (Scranton). There they soon far outnumbered those in the two largest counties in the south.

The earliest East European colony in the northern part of the anthracite area was formed at Nanticoke at just about the time of the one founded at Shamokin, and its importance rivals that of Shenandoah as a Polish center. It would grow into the most Polish town in the state, if not in America. Yet it, too, included Lithuanians and other East Europeans.

The Susquehanna Coal Company in the area probably brought in the first Wyoming-region Poles in 1869 from New York. In a short time the little community built St. Stanislaus Church, the mother Polish parish for the other thirteen in the region before 1903. To accommodate the incoming waves, two more Polish Catholic churches arose in Nanticoke in 1894 and 1901. The Lithuanians in town had no choice but to join them.[12]

Elsewhere in the northern field the two nationalities contributed to the creation of a parish at Plymouth in 1882, and at Pittston in 1885 the first strictly Lithuanian church still included five Polish families.[13] Similarly, Poles, Lithuanians, and Slovaks participated, in various combinations, in the development of parishes in Scranton, Glen Lyon, Mocanaqua, and Forest City between 1885 and 1892.[14]

The Lehigh field featured the same early Slavic communities with perhaps more definite subdivision later. The mother church for East Europeans on the north side,

St. Casimir's at Freeland, honors ten of the original four-teen founders in 1886 as Polish and Lithuanian, and a decade later the parish included Slovaks and Ukraini-ans.[15] At Hazleton proper, Slovaks began services in 1882 at their first parish, and Lithuanians and Poles formed their own parishes during the next few years. At Lans-ford, Poles went to the Slovak church, while at Sheppton, southwest of Hazleton, all Slavic Catholics attended St. Joseph's.[16]

Friction, when it did exist, cannot have been at all constant, as ethnic warfare did not continue after the establishment of a new church. While subdivision may have occasionally originated with violence, the hostility was not continuous. In small colonies Slovaks, Rutheni-ans, Poles, and Lithuanians attended the very same Catholic church in apparently harmonious association. They not only experienced similar social development but also understood each other's language, lived a similar existence, and worked at the same job. These nationali-ties had much more in common than later group com-mentators would admit.[17] What is most significant here is that at least the contact between the various East Euro-pean settlements must have been a close one particularly when a major crisis, such as a strike, occurred.

Additional evidence for general Slavic communality lay in the nearly uniform growth of the ethnic colony regardless of nationality.[18] First came the individual pio-neers, who through their letters encouraged their country-men to join them. When a large enough group had arrived, small, mutual-aid societies were formed to help in time of economic emergencies. These poorly organized groups made sporadic collections among the little colonies for sickness and death assistance, and in time these local associations spearheaded the drive to build a church, an important element of the old primary unit, the village, that the immigrants knew.

Thus most Polish and Lithuanian laborers looking for work before 1903 came to mature ethnic colonies, in most cases nationality parishes anxious to orient them and to help them pursue the quest for wealth that had brought them here. And they did succeed in winning their "bread."

The typical greenhorn would have alighted from the immigrant train in the Pennsylvania hard-coal region undoubtedly apprehensive if he had not yet met his correspondent. With luck, one or both had a photograph to aid in recognizing the other. Otherwise the weary traveler at the depot asked or shouted the name of his sponsor. One can imagine the tears of joy on both sides when to the immigrant's call his countryman responded, and their relief was expressed in a demonstrative embrace. "Certainly there is something touching in their predicament and it is remarked by all who saw them—alone in a strange country, unable to understand or make themselves understood . . . and not knowing which way to go." But when they found their people, "instantly their countenance was illuminated with unmistakeable joy and 'Dobra!' (Fine!) was grunted out as a sign of acquiescence."[19]

The sponsor then led his charge to a group of shacks

usually at the edge of town. This ghetto was separated from the rest of the populace, just as in other places in America where the East Europeans lived. Here in the coal country inhabitants termed the foreign nest the Slavic mining "patch." If he arrived at night, the bundle-laden traveler would have to grope through the darkness, as no street illumination, paved roads, or signs (even if he could have read them) facilitated this last, short trip.

Entering one of the houses, the arrival found it in some respects like the peasant cottage in Poland. Although mean, it provided both ethnic comfort and economic security. A countryman and his wife managed the crowded household, which ordinarily included other male boarders as well as the rest of the owner's family. And the newcomer felt even more at home when he discovered that this nucleus of the Slavic-American community even represented specific geographic sectors of the old country. In fact a similar housing arrangement flourished among all Slavs everywhere, Poles, Lithuanians, and others, who wanted an economical place to live—"trzymanie bortników," the boardinghouse system.

Admittedly all arrivals were not so fortunate; the Slavic pioneers of the 1870's and early 1880's encountered real hardships. A few fortunate ones roomed with sympathetic Germans. But elsewhere Irish and English landlords exploited these greenhorns, for example, by packing ten men and one woman into a one-room cellar, eleven feet square; or twenty-one in a two-storied stable, sixteen by fourteen; or six males in a windowless room, fourteen by nine.[20]

Such overcrowded conditions improved somewhat when Slavs began devising their own living arrangements. They accumulated enough money to buy or rent land on which to build a one-room shanty. Such quarters were erected cheaply with any scrap material available: railroad ties, timber, palings, driftwood, and empty tins. When more countrymen appeared, these pioneer builders became boarding house landlords by renting out quarters. The inhabitants per room soon increased, and the shanty itself expanded to two or more rooms with perhaps an attic or second floor.

Such an arrangement appealed to both tenant and landlord. The rent was low, yet the landlords made money. In the 1880's and 1890's Slavs in the anthracite area usually rented out their three- and four-room structures to four or five bachelors per room.[21] Thus receiving an income from fifteen or so boarders, some landlords could quit work at the mines, send home for their families, and devote their full time to their household.

The appearance of a patch was not very pleasant. Most of the structures, standing ten feet high and twenty-five feet square, were huddled together on small plots. The grey scrap wood was unpainted, as was the ever-present outhouse a short distance away. The peasants were no architects, and the conglomeration looked like a huge dump rather than a settlement. The hovels had roofs slanting in all directions, with eaves and without, sides of different lengths, and windows of various sizes appearing helter-skelter in the walls. Uneven, fenced enclosures and doors of varying lengths finished the jumble. The shacks not only looked like a large dump but also smelled like one. All about lay mounds of garbage and alley offal. The odors of this refuse and of open sewers filled the air. As late as 1916 only a few anthracite towns had a paved street or regular garbage collection. The exceptional community cleared its open-vault privy twice a year.

The appearance of the huts probably gave the non-Slav the picture of chronic poverty. But the inhabitants were not poor; they accepted such conditions for maximum income, "za chlebem." The immigrant mineworker spent little of his income on furnishings. Many quarters had neither ceilings nor floors. Like those in the old country, the normal household was spare, with at most a stove, table, chests, and benches. Crowded everywhere were beds, protruding from the walls and giving the impression of a dilapidated dormitory. If the structure did have an upper story, it was usually little more than a loft holding additional sleepers. Privacy, then, in the Slavic boardinghouse was unknown.

The room-and-board costs for new immigrants were universally low. The common method of payment evolved with the growth of the shanty itself. Generally after getting a job, the boarder would give the landlord a certain amount for supplying his bed, food, and other services.

In the beginning tenants slept on the floor, contributed funds to a common store, and designated one to buy supplies, do household chores, and serve as cook. That arrangement at best was unsatisfactory, but throughout the late 1800's this all-male living existed in the newer settlements. As the communities matured, the growing number of Slavic women considerably eased life for the men. The wife of the boardinghouse landlord aided her mate as a hard-working housekeeper, and she added much to keeping the living expense low for all. On any normal day the patch visitor might find her carrying water from the only source for the settlement, a common hydrant perhaps some distance away. Or one might see her tending a nearby mound, the patch's communal bakeoven. For the Slav at least two of life's staples, bread and water, were cheap.

Unfortunately the fanatic drive to economize forced the immigrant woman into a tragic role; she served her male companions almost as a slave. While her husband collected rent, she cooked, washed, and kept house for the tenants, and in addition to these tasks had her own large family to raise. It is no wonder that Slavic women aged quickly. They were valued far more for their contribution to family wealth than for their companionship, and their only other function was to bear children with what has been called a reckless fecundity.[22] The female's continuing peasant status was criticized by American observers, especially in regard to the apparently frequent beatings which the husband inflicted. The kerchiefed wife shocked nativists, who often saw her barefoot, chopping wood or atop culm piles gathering coal waste in her skirt.

Part of the reason for desiring many children was the economical help they offered. When very young, they assisted the exhausted mother with chores; and when older, they went out to work. Girls usually got jobs in the local textile mills, while the boys had to labor at the mines. Of course, on payday all Polish American youth were expected to pool their earnings with those of the rest of their family.

Food costs also were kept to a minimum. The meals which the wife prepared cost much less than those of ordinary Americans. The fare had improved over that in in Europe, but it was still cheap and monotonous. Cereals and starches, potatoes and bread, provided the chief staples; meat appeared on the table often, but the immigrants bought the cheapest cuts and scraps for boiling, with perhaps a "green" shoulder of pork. Black bread, coffee, and oily fish completed their menu. Without vegetables in their diet, except for cabbage, they suffered occasionally from deficient nutrition, and scurvy at times swept through their settlements.

One store in Schuylkill County showed the average expense for Slavs to be $2.86 per capita per month, while the Anglo-Saxons paid almost twice that ($5.48).[23] Also, buying at stores run by proprietors of their own nationality may have helped, at least by the turn of the century.

The providential Slav had ways of obtaining food and fuel without paying for them. The former peasants did not hesitate to grow their own food. Despite the small land parcels on which the dwellings stood, almost every East European, those in boardinghouses as well as those in private households, worked a plot into a vegetable garden. Such small-scale cultivation was common on adjacent open ground or at the edge of the colony.

The immigrant also raised livestock, perhaps a cow, a few chickens, or a goat, just as in the old country.

For fuel the immigrant in winter collected the nearby driftwood and culm, which the coal company supplied cheaply. Clothing, too, was hardly a problem. Second-hand merchants kept the community well supplied cheaply.[24] The omnipresence of half-naked children and shoeless women also attested to the low cost of family garments.

The total cost of living, then, for single Slavs in the anthracite region was undoubtedly low in the last years of the century. About 1890, for example, the average boarder could exist on approximately ten dollars a month.[25]

Of course the Poles, Lithuanians, and Slovaks also expended some of their income on other, culturally necessary items, their churches and their saloons. In fact, in a strange land the former peasant first sought security with his fellows by supporting self-help societies. It was these mutual aid groups which organized the parish.

Despite the uprooting, the immigrant in America and his children as well took their Catholicism seriously, and the young greenhorn eating his first meal as a member of the boardinghouse system was undoubtedly comforted by the gaudy, gilded representation of the Crucifixion, the Virgin, or some other sacred theme reminding him of home. "The religious attitudes prove . . . the most lasting of all traditional components of the peasants' social psychology. They remain strong even in the second generation of immigrants in [the United States]."[26]

While the earlier arrivals perhaps were most devoted, for all the church remained an object of awe and love. A long walk, perhaps even miles, for the anthracite-area Poles to hear Mass in their own tongue by their own priests was not uncommon. For the parish was more than a place of worship; it was the center of Polonia, the Polish community in America, and the force that perpetuated "Polskość" (Polishness). Perhaps more than for any other ethnic group, nationality and religion were synonymous; to be Polish meant to be Catholic.

The Poles regarded the individual who symbolized religiousness, the priest, with profound respect and humility. The authority of this leader in the old country extended far, and both Poles and outsiders reemphasized his power here over his flock. The cleric was not just a religious director but a teacher, adviser, and mediator as well. However, if the situation in the anthracite region is any criterion, the priest's influence in nonclerical matters, as labor unrest, was not decisive.

The American parish alone could not replace the primary, self-contained village entirely. There were important differences. Church members came from a broader geographic area than in the old country and undoubtedly even included non-Poles. In addition a new force, mutual self-help, had built the parish and was maintaining it in a country which separated Church and state. Still another institution was needed to bind the several Slavic nationalities and parishes in a freer social atmosphere, and the saloon filled this need.

Upon leaving church on a Sunday, the Pole may well

47

have gone to this other mainstay of the community. The former peasant, indeed, loved his liquor, and Anglo-Americans did not always appreciate his thirst. One commentator, Reverend Peter Roberts, condemned the bacchanalian Polish orgies, found especially at weddings and christenings. He quoted a friend's description of the usual Sabbath desecration: " 'It was terrible; saloons full blast; singing and dancing and drinking everywhere; it was Sodom and Gomorrah revived; the judgment of God, sir, will fall upon us.' "[27]

But the saloons and the nationality stores served a less obvious function: exchange centers for the ethnic settlements. The proprietors, usually German Poles, had been the earliest arrivals, and, seeing the need for a neighborhood center, they invested in a local establishment. They and their saloons did provide necessary services, such as holding the immigrants' earnings—the so-called "immigrant banks"—notarizing papers, forwarding money orders home, acting as transportation agents, affording accomodations, interpreting and translating, giving generous credit to countrymen, and even writing letters for the illiterate. Their business hours were convenient, and the interested parties conducted negotiations over lager.

Shopkeepers, then, wielded considerable local influence, and many acted as mediators and spokesmen for their countrymen. Carl Rice, the Lithuanian clothing merchant of Shenandoah; John Nemeth, the Polish grocer and transportation agent from Hazleton; Emil Malinowski, the Polish brewer and banker of Nanticoke; and John Kosek, the Slovak grocer of Wilkes-Barre—all rose to prominence in these commercial pursuits, and, as the reader will see, took an active role in labor affairs.

The most important function of the anthracite district saloon was as a labor exchange. If the immigrant arrived unsponsored or was just looking for employment, he went to the neighborhood public house. It was here that foremen and employers knew they could get the eager, unskilled labor they desired.

On the novice's first day of work in the mine fields, the housewife would have been up long before the town arose to the six o'clock whistle at the mine.[28] In addition to preparing the breakfast, she usually packed the dinner pails for everyone. She also dressed and fed her children, some of whom themselves may have worked at the mine. If the men were lucky, the railroad company provided free rail or trolley service from the settlement to the workplace. Or it may have charged a small fee. Otherwise the workers walked the two or three miles to get to the mine before seven.

The sight of so many children employed in mining along with their fathers appalled many Americans. The Slav would give a ready answer when accused of practising child labor—economic necessity. Popular American abhorrence of the evil forced through minimum age laws, but to little avail, as parents and employers violated them with rare penalty. Some child labor reformers announced that they had found boys as young as six working at the mines; nine or ten, however, was probably the actual minimum. A leading reformer sympathized with the East

European youngster as the "helpless victim of the frugality, ignorance, and industrial instincts of his parents."[29] The value placed by Americans on educating the young little interested the Slav, for the valuable child was the working one. Above a minimum, education was useless, and the pressing need for income forced sons into the pits at or before their teens.

At the mine the littlest ones worked in the huge, eighty-foot breaker, the "nursery" some named it. This structure in operation presented a terrifying sight to the uninitiated. The coal rushing down the chutes made a deafening roar and sent up clouds of coal dust everywhere. Once the visitor accustomed himself to the haze, he would have to peer through the greyness to see the inmates, young boys seated on boards bent over chutes. From time to time they operated a shutter which regulated the flow, and then they picked out slate to separate it from the coal. The air at times would grow to a choking thickness, but the boys would work on while their supervisor, leaning on a switch, stood above them. In this nursery, too, strangely enough, one could find bent old men working alongside the youths. They had spent their manhood underground, and, broken and worn out, they had now returned to the surface for the rest of their days. So the breaker could have been termed a home for the elderly as well. All of the workers here, men and boys, labored the normal ten-hour day, six-day week, when at full time.

The Slav in the prime of life conducted his work belowground in the mine itself. The former Slavic plowboy going down in the elevator for the first time was surely upset by the rapid descent into utter darkness. Alighting at the bottom and walking toward his chamber, he could just make out headlamp flashes and flitting shadows. He may well have noticed youngsters not much older than the breaker boys accompanying him along the gangway.

Increasingly, then, the total mining operation for the worker took on the appearance of a "school." From the surface at about twelve years of age, boys in their midteens graduated underground to tending doors along the gangway which regulated ventilation. Older teenagers moved on to the position of mule leaders and keepers, then drivers hauling coal, until at maturity they, like most average Slavs, worked as miners' helpers.[30] If lucky, some Poles became "miners," but a required examination after 1889 restricted them somewhat.

Slavs, then, were breaker boys, miner's helpers, or occasionally miners. Few worked in the skilled and supervisory positions of foreman, pumpman, engineer, fireman, or carpenter.[31]

When the day drew to a close, the laborer would likely find himself alone in the underground room. Since the miner pulled down the black rock faster than his assistant could load it, he frequently went home long before the loading was done. It was the rare miner who labored the full ten hours. He usually departed no later than three or four, to leave the assistant to do the remaining tasks, complete the loading, clear the refuse to the side, and prepare the area for the next day's work. The weary Slavic mineworkers trudged home after sunset, keeping their headlamps lit to find their way. Each completed his day at home with a good bath to restore his skin to its natural color.

The grueling work continued day after day, but the East European looked forward eagerly to payday. The miners and breaker boys usually received a daily or monthly salary direct from the company, but the mine laborers usually received their money from the miner. The miner hired or subcontracted the Pole or Lithuanian, who thus was his employee rather than the operator's.

Two broad practices of compensating miners were common, "by-the-run," the lineal distance worked in the mine, or "by-the-wagon," the number of cars filled. The wagon system produced considerable protest, as the percentage of waste in the load was calculated arbitrarily by the company. The weighman had a tendency to dock the miner unfairly, and the sizes of the cars varied.

Despite semimonthly salary acts of 1881, 1887, and 1891, almost every operator compensated his men once a month. At first receiving their pay in credit slips on local stores, after about 1860 most workers took it in cash. A contract miner would take his immigrant helper to the nearby saloon, where he would give the Slav a third of his salary.

The amounts that the Slavic mineworker received generally drifted downward in the late 1800's. Averages about 1870 were $3.00 per day for miners, $2.00 for general laborers, and $.80 for breaker boys.[32] By the end of the century the three figures slipped to $2.25, $1.40, and $.75.[33]

In the Lehigh open-pit strippings the Polish, Italian, and Slovak employees of the independent operators were in a worse way. They found their pay about one-third less than that of their countrymen to the north and south. Markle, Pardee, and others deducted sums for workers' churches and purchases at the company-owned stores, and the latter charges were at times excessive.[34]

Pay Slip for Slavic Miner*

No. . . . .   Hazleton, Pa., Nov. 30, 1897

Name . . . .

IN ACCOUNT WITH A. PARDEE & CO.

By Balance
" 69 Cars at $1.18 Cr. $81.42

To Balance
" Powder 13.75
" Cutting Timber . . . .
" Smithing 38
" Laborer 30.75
" Rent 4.50
" Coal . . . .
" Merchandise 7.49
" Board . . . .
" Doctor 50

                                                     57.37

                                                  $24.05

* From CBS, "The Coal Miners' Strike," *The Outlook*, LXVI (September 27, 1900), 256.

Thus the accumulation of the wealth the immigrant sought could not have been easy. Did he find what he came for? Dedicated to a goal, working incredibly hard, was he really able to accumulate savings? Undoubtedly some Slavs failed in trying to earn sufficient money for economic security, but by and large most mineworkers succeeded despite the small pittance and company deductions. In addition to their nearly superhuman sense of thrift another trait helped the Slavs to earn the money for which they had come—their mobility.

The immigrant's ability to move staved off disaster during local economic crises. Upon a shutdown of the mines or the periodic reductions in production, the mobile Slavic bachelor left quickly for a less-affected sector of industrial America. Or, with his family, he could return to Europe temporarily, to retrace his steps when conditions improved. Having made the journey once, the immigrant knew that he could cross the ocean with few real complications.

Observers report unanimously of the Slavs' economic success through succeeding periods of settlement. According to Balch, immediately after the East European's arrival he got a job, an American suit, a trunk for a locker, and a watch—and then started depositing his money.[35] And a local figure described an influx of immigrants to his mining town: "They came not for conscience sake—they came for money, and *they are getting it*."[36] A Lithuanian wrote of families that he knew: "Great frugality and . . . saving were some of the cardinal virtues which foreign-born parents with considerable

54

perseverance attempted to inculcate into their native-born children."[37]

Others noticed similar characteristics. Terence V. Powderly, the United States Immigration Commissioner, probably exaggerated when he complained that Hungarians in the anthracite area spent only fifteen cents of every dollar, but a storekeeper who dealt with them told a reporter that except for bad whiskey they avoided luxuries. According to one report, living cost them fifty cents a day, and they saved at least half of their yearly four hundred dollars.[38] A prominent Pole and two correspondents familiar with the mineworkers also agreed that the Slavs held onto about one-half of their income.[39]

The growing wealth of the immigrants, living in their overcrowded shanties, must have amazed English-speaking neighbors, who on their part "were glad to squander their . . . wages on material comforts."[40] Less than a decade after establishing their early parish at Shenandoah, the Polish laborers there held one hundred thousand dollars worth of assessed property, adding half again as much two years later. By 1900 the Lithuanians alone in Shenandoah could boast of wealth totaling a third of a million dollars. The 2 million dollars of mineworkers' deposits in Wilkes-Barre banks at that time was about as much as was in the banks of Polish Nanticoke. The Slovaks, who came later to the region, also could save. Their major savings bank in Hazleton at the start of World War I possessed over eight hundred thousand dollars.[41]

These local riches did not include the large stream of money orders that was sent back from America to Old-

World villages year after year. A writer in the early 1880's summed up the habits of Poles and probably Lithuanians in Shenandoah briefly: "They are a very saving class of people, and . . . have proved their ability to live at much less cost than any other nationality among us." He supported his contention with the fact that they sent about ten thousand dollars per month to the old country.[42] A "reasonable calculation" of eastward remittances about that time from the Lehigh area would be more than one hundred thousand dollars per year.[43] Italians and Slavs probably sent well over five times that much at the turn of the century.[44]

Undoubtedly some Poles did return with loaded money bags to reestablish themselves at home. But most, having dug into the American Eldorado, decided to remain and bring over their families. They had not forgotten their love for the soil, however, and a new incentive took hold—to purchase real estate here in America. Charles Coulter expressed the new goal best: "The Pole is unique in that he is not a renter. . . . He never loses the intense desire engendered through generations of peasant life to own a house and a lot. . . . With the first . . . paid for, immediately he invests in another property."[45] In a survey of Shenandoah, Mt. Carmel, Nanticoke, and Olyphant, Dr. Roberts found that the Slavs held over 2½ million dollars worth of real estate, or one hundred dollars per capita. He concluded that their quest for land in the last fifteen years of the century was surprising considering the high real estate prices.[46]

With this sound financial base, then, the Poles' good

sense of organization gave the finishing touches to their communities in northeastern Pennsylvania by the last decade of the century. Slavic building and loan associations were thriving. The many local societies had affiliated with strong national organizations, like the clerical Polish Roman Catholic Union of Chicago, the Polish Union of Buffalo and Wilkes-Barre, and the gymnastic Falcons of Pittsburgh and other semimilitary groups. The small colonies boasted at least six Polish newspaper starts, half of which functioned for at least five consecutive years before 1901. Polish singing societies and nationality bands formed and prospered. And the larger towns began to notice a tiny group of Slavs in the professions just before 1903.

The Poles and other East Europeans thus had won their place in the anthracite field in the short space of a generation. A few, of course, suffered from the migration, but only rarely was a Slavic immigrant destroyed by the move. The Slavic communities, either mixed or homogeneous ethnic societies, helped the newcomers to adjust by providing facilities to ease any cultural shock. The mainstays of the neighborhood—the boardinghouse, church, and saloon—allowed the newcomer to obtain what he came for, inexpensive living and remunerative employment, with some ethnic and cultural continuity.

The story of this community construction is one of success in terms of the Slavs' desires. Demanding little for comfort, "kenneled like dogs," as one American described it, these families and bachelors labored tirelessly at home and in the mines and attained their goal,

57

economic security. They certainly won the cottage or parcel of land denied them in the old country, as nearly all made material progress.

The advanced community organization and penny-pinching economy were to affect the anthracite industry, especially the relations between capital and labor. American workers at first ignored the new immigrants' appearance, and the new groups did not attract notice until after 1880. Unaware of the community's function and the immigrant's quest for bread, labor reformers to the 1890's had little information on how the East European would regard his employer. Would he be submissive, docile, and passive toward the operators? Or would he be willing to sacrifice income temporarily in strikes and respond to the exhortations of union missionaries? Unfortunately, in the early organizing activity labor leaders still had no sure answer to the puzzle.

IV

Early Union Failures

SOCIETY DOES NOT TREAT REFORMERS KINDLY. THE NATUral tendency of man supports the status quo and even under intolerable circumstances moves slowly to change. Only a small minority, upon seeing supposed inequities, will dissent or sacrifice their positions to take remedial action.

In nineteenth-century America only a few urged workingmen to organize and counter capital's power. Many objected to unfair working conditions, but rarely did leaders attempt to persuade workers to use their collective strength through union; only a dedicated handful worked for industrial democracy as an immediate goal. Knowing the obstacles before them in the anthracite districts would have made even these men less sanguine, for pitfalls existed within the movement as well as without.

The Slavic Community on Strike

Reviewing industrial unrest to 1880, the labor advocate would have had little to cheer about. Few organizations survived from early union history, and those remaining were weak, miserable affairs, merely small colliery locals. The grand designs of organizers for industrywide combinations in 1848, 1868, and 1877 were only briefly successful and in the end failed.

Why organization was not permanent in the third quarter of the century is a question which must be examined, for the reasons for failure are significant. They not only indicate the relevance of East Europeans to American unions but also expose a more important deficiency in the organization of the anthracite workers, a deficiency that would plague labor agitators to the end of the century. What were the flaws in hard-coal labor unionization? The answer is, not naivete and resistance to organization on the part of the Slavic immigrants, but rather faulty union strategy combined with operator intransigence.

The thesis that the waves of Slavic entrants killed unions, while an old one, still has never been countered. In fact, the image of hordes of docile, ignorant Slavs and Italians, being led dumbly into the fields by crafty operators to break strikes, continues to hang over the anthracite region. One authority has described the feeling of disappointed unionists in the 1890's: "The recollection that these [East European] foreigners . . . had been imported as strikebreakers by the thousands during and after the last strikes of '75 and '77, was wormwood and gall to the older [nationalities]."[1] And another reporter more exactly pinpointed the demise of labor. For him the blow was struck during the so-called Long Strike of 1875 when "one of the greatest of operators sent abroad to Austria-Hungary and brought thence to his mining patch [a boatload of peasants], the first of the foreigners." These shortly "succeeded in driving out" many of the English-speaking miners.[2] A contemporary student of immigration concurred: "The Slavs . . . were introduced into Pennsylvania forty odd years ago [about 1875 or before] . . . frequently . . . when a strike was on."[3] A recent student of skilled Welsh anthracite miners has carried this idea even further. He stated that the introduction of unskilled East Europeans with the Irish and Germans in the 1870's as strikebreakers "resulted in unionization . . . becoming a matter of some difficulty."[4]

These observers, then, appear to refer to two major labor disputes which new immigrants were believed to have affected significantly, the Long Strike of 1875 and the unrest of 1877. This ethnic view, however, obscures the more important economic and political character of these incidents. Both major disputes which erupted in the period, the WBA efforts of the early 1870's and the riots of 1877, clearly had little to do with new immigrants. The reasons for their failure were very similar to the problems encountered in later organizing efforts: a militant employer resistance and insufficiently coordinated union strategy. The tripartite division of the industry into Wyoming, Lehigh, and Schuylkill fields was a feature too difficult for labor leaders to overcome in their attempts to unify. They were not able to enforce their decisions uniformly to maximize the workers' economic power.

To the end of the Civil War no one had yet created

any industrywide labor association. Only loosely connected local bodies had emerged, like the Bates Union of 1848, the Forestville Union of 1860, the Miners' Benevolent Society of Locust Gap, the Archbald Benevolent Association of 1863, the Benevolent Society of Carbon County in 1864, and the Workingmen's Benevolent Association (WBA) of St. Clair of 1868.[5]

The head of the St. Clair body, John Siney, was the man to consolidate these local groups into an all-inclusive organization. Unfortunately, however, his success was all too short. Siney's organizational qualities had originated from a very relevant past. An immigrant from Ireland, he had been engaged in the British Isles in forming labor groups before coming to America. Upon his arrival here it appeared that his organizational philosophy became much more conservative. He felt that the unions in the anthracite industry ought to work with the operators rather than against them. Together labor and capital ought to eliminate the bane of a glutted market.[6]

Whether it was Siney's fundamental acceptance of capitalism that attracted mineworkers or his organizational and personal magnetism, the fact is that his WBA grew quickly in 1868. Great numbers of southern district miners flocked to the union within the year. Local wage reductions and the operators' refusal to abide by a recent eight-hour-day law further aggravated discontent. Obviously the men's motives in joining were more belligerent than Siney's, but the leader capitalized on their dissatisfaction. He sent organizers outside of Schuylkill, north into the other two fields. The union increased its strength by dominating the General Council in March, 1869, a meeting at which mineworking labor bodies in all six anthracite counties were represented.[7] By mid-1869, after some setbacks, the WBA leaders could boast of having recruited 85 percent of the total anthracite work force. It seemed that a formidable economic power had emerged.

Another indication of labor's might appeared in politics. With its new-found influence the WBA proceeded to force the enactment of favorable legislation, especially by effecting the passage of important inspection and protective measures from 1869 to 1875. Perhaps the most significant of these came in 1875 in a law that the men had sought for some time. The measure partially regulated the determination of the miners' pay by permitting the union to select a check-weighman at the breaker to assure that the accounting was fair.[8]

Certainly the operators would have to concede that a strong labor organization was apparent by 1870. There is little need here to go into the details of labor unrest in the years until the demise of the WBA in the first half of 1875.[9] The operator-employee contact in that period alternated between bitterness and collusion in work suspensions in order to reduce coal supplies. Various arrangements for industrial peace were devised, like the so-called sliding scale after the 1869 strike and the Gowen Compromise of 1870, the basis for wage adjustment to 1874.[10] The two most important features of industrial relations were, first, that by 1874 the WBA still seemed to be a strong organization, yet, second, the body suffered from significant weaknesses.[11]

Before 1874 two limitations, one within and the other without the WBA, caused its decline in that period, and these were to handicap unionization for more than two decades: one was the inability of the union to control the entire anthracite work force and the other was the rising hostility of management.

The internal problem was especially debilitating. The union was often unable to enforce its discipline evenly in the three fields; there was too much jealousy and dissension among the men. When one field wanted to lay down its tools for some grievance, another did not; and even when all did go out, each would return at different times, thus to sabotage the strike of the other.[12]

The northern field, the farthest from the WBA's stronghold in Schuylkill, acted most independently. The Wyoming area in the beginning consisted of the fewer and larger coal producers even less receptive to work force organization than those elsewhere. The two 1868 strikes in Schuylkill, one in July and the other in December, found some organized following in Lehigh but almost none around Scranton. The General Council's call out of May, 1869, was more successful and did get universal support. But the unanimity was both delayed and short-lived, for those northern men who did finally strike went out one month later and returned after two months to terms different from those of their southern neighbors, a pay increase instead of the sliding scale. The employees of one large northern operator, the Pennsylvania Coal Company, never did stop work. In the next large strike, in 1870, only the Schuylkill men went out.

The northern lethargy annoyed those to the south, and the southern workers retaliated later in the year. When the Wyoming companies threatened a large pay cut, their men struck and asked the WBA for general support. The Schuylkill men had their own contract and opposed such a suspension, but the union leaders called one anyway in January, 1871.[13] The reluctant southerners returned within a month, to force the Wyoming miners to surrender a short time later. The WBA's order to each field to make the best terms possible really killed unionism in the upper region for more than a decade.

Along with its inability to direct all fields to advantage, the union faced a second obstacle, the external one of capital. Labor's opponents had increasingly resented the WBA between 1870 and 1874. Franklin B. Gowen, president of the Reading, was trying to weld the many Schuylkill producers into a monolithic combination under his railroad. In fact most of the lower-area carriers had joined, and in December of 1874 they challenged the workers with wage reductions as high as 20 percent. When the WBA, now called the Miners' and Laborers' Benevolent Association, refused to agree and struck early in January, the issue was joined.

Bitter memories are attached to the contest of those next six months, the so-called Long Strike of 1875. This industrial conflict is worthy of close study to uncover the reasons for a once-powerful labor body, engaged in serious combat, to lose so badly. The two basic weaknesses were apparent early, determined operators insisting upon wage cuts, and an ineffective union. Labor leaders could get only part of the men to strike. Those who did go out suspended work at different times after January 1, when the Schuylkill men struck. Normal coal production continued at Hazleton until late that month and around Shamokin until early April.[14] Except for the workers around Wilkes-Barre, most of the northerners accepted the reduction and continually ignored southerners' pleas to follow them.[15]

By April the struggle centered mainly in the Lehigh and Schuylkill districts and settled down to a grim conflict with occasional violence. At that time, after property had been fired and nonunion men attacked, the Governor ordered several hundred troops to Hazleton, where the outbreaks were most serious.[16]

MLBA President Welsh publicly appealed to his men to avoid any participation in lawless activities. But hungry men do not heed pleas for caution. After one of the first property assaults a reporter declared: "The desperation of the miners' strike is only just beginning. Where it will end heaven only knows."[17] Welsh's compromise offers in the last months after April were ignored by a defiant operators' committee which refused to budge from its original reduction.

Occasional stonings of coal trains, attacks on hired police, and marches on operating mines continued until the men, seeing no hope for negotiations, weakened by the end of May, after five months of idleness. An observer of the Schuylkill surrender lamented: "The destitution of many of the families of the miners and laborers is pitiable, and it will take the labor of years to regain the loss suffered by this county during the long strike just ended."[18] Though the Lehigh men remained out, their compatriots to the south drifted back to work. By June the backbone of the strike was broken; MLBA leaders at Pottsville ran up the white flag on June 14 by ordering the men to return whenever they wished. While the battle was done, some yielded reluctantly, particularly the more resistant Lehigh strikers, who did not surrender until early July. Unionism in the anthracite region was to be the exception rather than the rule for the next twelve years.

The historian, in seeking reasons for labor's defeat in these early strikes, would have to ascribe the crushing loss primarily to the employers. With their severe wage cuts and refusal to negotiate, the operators signaled their determination to kill the union, and the union's response, the strike, was self-defense.

The second most important factor, sectional jealousy, was not cured by MLBA organization. Despite unity pleas, the Delaware and Hudson and the Delaware, Lackawanna and Western men continued to work and undercut the strength of the MLBA. The booming coal production in the north irritated the other sections as it was obviously sabotaging their strike effort and seizing their share of the market. Strike leaders did try to obtain the northerners' active support but were unsuccessful, only stimulating the resentment of their followers. After a visit to working collieries in Luzerne, President Welsh himself admitted his deep disappointment at the apathy of the Luzerne men. As a result of this failure, strikers

67

vented their frustration over their officials. As one despaired when the struggle was coming to a close:

> My family and I must have something to eat and I am too proud to beg and too honest to rob. At other regions they are reaping a rich harvest and enjoy the pleasure of seeing us idle, because they cannot sell their inferior coal when better coal, such as ours, can be got. Three years ago our leaders trusted to the integrity of the Luzerne men, and before they knew what was transpiring, Luzerne was in full blast of actual work, and after having been out for three long months, everyone (here in Schuylkill) was glad to resume work for less than we struck. . . . Now we are having a case almost equally as bad.[19]

What apparently was needed here and thereafter was a militant disciplinary force which would insure strike loyalty in all three fields. By the turn of the century it would be found in the East European community. Gowen, president of the Reading, took chief credit for the victory of the operators. As early as March he warned his men that union membership meant immediate dismissal.[20] As the largest operator, he announced later that he had spent an immense sum on guards and detectives during the strike to break it. The Wyoming mineowner affected, Charles Parrish, also gave his men no quarter. He forced strikers from their company homes and refused to rehire them without individual contracts.

The Schuylkill union proclaimed its demise in a postmortem: "Mr. Gowen and the operators of Schuylkill County have the satisfaction of knowing that as a county organization, we can continue the fight no longer; that the keen pangs of hunger have driven the more unfortunate of our members into the reluctant acceptance of terms which, under other circumstances, they could never have been induced to accept."[21] A strike leader's recollection agreed: "Hunger forced the men to yield . . . The Miners' and Laborers' Benevolent Association was broken."[22]

The question of the role of national groups, particularly the East Europeans, remains. A few Slavs at this time had already begun to settle in western Schuylkill at Shamokin, Shenandoah, and Mt. Carmel, as well as at Nanticoke in Wyoming. But by and large their part was passive. Ethnic origins may have influenced the result, but nearly all sources refer to union members as Irish, Welsh, English, and German rather than Slavic. The West European nationalities during the conflict did not always agree on union policy; some voted to return while others insisted on holding out. Observers particularly singled out the Irish for antiemployer terrorism, particularly through the supposedly secret Hibernian "Molly Maguires."[23] Had the "Hungarians" made any impact on the struggle in any way, publicists certainly would have broadcast such activity. But the new immigrants did not at that time make their presence known.

Contrary to legend, no freight loads of "pauper labor" rushed in to fill strikers' places. The importation of non-strikers did produce some conflict, but such clashes were minor and no particular nationality was involved. For example, one individual from Philadelphia told of his being recruited with others as guards. But when they were ordered to work in the mines, they refused and were

69

stranded.[24] Other evidence consisted of a widespread rumor of an influx of Italian scabs. This allegation, however, was only partly valid. The imports of this nationality turned out to be a group sent into the Clearfield soft-coal field to break a strike there.[25]

Of course, it is true that many workers, including Slavs, ignored the union appeal and continued working, but a study of the struggle in the most heavily East European localities reveals no particular bias for or against unionism on the part of the immigrants at this time. What was the reaction of the Slavs in the areas of their most concentrated settlement?

Nanticoke area workers of the Susquehanna and the Lehigh and Wilkes-Barre heeded the union call and did not return to work until mid-June. At Shenandoah all men, immigrant and native, acted together and returned to work about the same time. The only large-scale mining operation in which Slavs may have participated took place in Shamokin in west Schuylkill. There, infrequent shutdowns interrupted normal production. On the whole probably a good part of the Slavic handful followed the MLBA's lead, and the Shamokin exception contributed little to labor's defeat. Indeed, "hunkies" were just too few to be significant.[26]

While the Long Strike of 1875 killed the Benevolent Association and proscribed organization for some time, labor conflict did break out again just two years later in an incident that provides another example for analysis of motive and nationality participation. The investigator once again searches in vain for evidence that ethnic origins affected workers' resistance.

In essence, the origins of the conflict in 1877 came not from union agitation but from difficult economic conditions. Unions were hardly in evidence. The hard times of the mid-1870's seeded the ground for discontent as the depression hit the anthracite region especially hard, to bring low prices and unemployment. With no strong union as their foil, the operators now could recoup their losses at will. At least twice, in 1876 and again in 1877, they lowered wages 10 to 15 percent.[27]

At first the impoverished workers took the cut silently. But violence stemming from want soon appeared likely. The visible signs of poverty frightened an observer in the spring of 1877: "The extent of destitution prevailing throughout the coal fields is assuming alarming proportions."[28] Bread riots seemed imminent.

Such violence did break out, erupting first in Scranton and reverberating southward. For there, where the work had continued in 1875, conditions had been the worst.[29] The city already had experienced minor labor unrest as a result of a nationwide railroad dispute. The rolling-mill workers of the Lackawanna Iron and Coal Company turned the disturbance into a strike at noon on July 23. Retaliating against a pay cut the week before, they now demonstrated for an increase. Unemployed railroad men and mineworkers of the DL and W rallied to the ironworkers' aid. The dissatisfaction spread to the Delaware and Hudson employees, and the crisis mounted. Three days later a mass meeting of strikers made the demand even stronger. Government authorities, having already suspected anarchists and revolutionaries, now took firm action. The workers' halting of trains forced

71

Governor Hartranft to ask President Hayes for troops. In addition, the Scranton mayor and a citizens' committee formed a small home guard of war veterans to maintain the peace.[30]

These precautions seemed to discourage strikers. The bewildered city executive, McKune, breathed easier on the thirtieth when some Lackawanna workers agreed to pump out the flooded mines and resume railroad service. Ominously, however, idle hands still milled about the streets.

Major violence occurred on August 1. The mayor tried to stop some marching strikers and was clubbed for his effort. Prostrate, he called for aid. The citizens' posse responded by firing into the demonstrators, killing three and wounding many more. Blood had been shed, and only the arrival of three thousand militia the next day quashed further demonstrations.

But the troops' entrance did not end the strike. Indeed, suspensions had occurred over all the region as the unemployed and underpaid mineworkers saw a way out of their misery. By the time of the shooting all of the Wyoming and Lehigh mines and the independent operators of Schuylkill were shut down. The major exception was the Reading, where President Gowen thanked his men for their loyalty.[31]

As the summer waned, men gradually returned to work, but not entirely in defeat. The earliest back on the job were in Lehigh, where workers had made their point. The local operators had to rehire them at the old wage, not the proposed reduction. The northern strikers followed a month later, and some were also offered better terms. The Wilkes-Barre contingent, for example, readily accepted President Parrish's 10 percent increase as did the Pittston men in early October.

However, the agitators at the D and H, DL and W, and the other mines of Wyoming now learned the humiliation of defeat as the WBA had in 1875. On October 16 the northern-area employees voted to go back at company terms. One week later the Lackawanna completed its triumph by firing fifty leading strikers.

This time, in 1877, labor leaders could salvage a few hopeful signs; some of the men successfully resisted pay cuts and even received raises. But many others did not, and unionism as the institution that it was in 1875 did not revive. The reason for this failure is as clear as it was two years before. Here the strikes were spontaneous outbursts. Starvation, not organization, was the cause. The few organized groups, like the Miners' Association of Scranton and the Knights of Labor District 5, while sympathetic, discountenanced violence, and their attempt at resurrecting the WBA met with little success.[32]

Now it was the northern men who were aggrieved, but they could not interest most of the south in a common cause. Certainly the refusal of the Schuylkill men must have disappointed the Wyoming strikers. Apparently the power of the Reading, the nightmare of the Long Strike, and the memory of Wyoming's unfriendliness in 1875 barred many southerners from joining their brothers.

A letter from a southern worker at the height of the conflict replied to northern appeals for a united front.

He dwelled upon the traditional distrust and claimed he had

> very good reason to doubt the loyalty of the Luzerne men to the Schuylkill men. Judging the future by the past, . . . the men of Luzerne want (us) to hold the cow while they milk her. . . . It would not be the first time they had played that trick. The writer of this knows whereof he speaks.

In addition, near the strike's end in the fall some Wyoming men even helped to kill their own cause by going south to work.[33]

The employers' attitude was another effective obstacle to workers' goals in the cases where the men lost. The continued hostility of the Scranton operators was similar to the 1875 intransigence of the Schuylkill companies and finally led to defeat. With widespread begging at the D and H mines, it clearly was desperation that caused the surrender of workers there.[34]

Once again the East European groups counted for little in the outcome, even if a slightly more significant number of Slavs now lived in the region. For example, Slavs were still so few that a local Scranton figure neglected them entirely in a list of mineworkers arranged according to ethnic origin.[35] Another authority insisted that immigrants had no part in the affairs of the 1870's since few had come to Wyoming by then.[36] The Lithuanians did not appear in Scranton until the year following the strike, 1878, and Polish settlement was too small to support a church before 1885.

Elsewhere already established Slavic colonies made no

particular impression on the course of the struggle. The recent peasants did not act independently but apparently went along with their fellows. A riot did erupt in Shamokin after a meeting of out-of-work mineworkers demanding "employment or something to eat," but the strike there was not defeated by immigrant scabs. In a rare mention of Poles by the local press, the opinion was expressed that their behavior aided the strikers. In August over one hundred left with much fanfare for work in the Illinois soft-coal fields.[37]

At another East European center, Shenandoah, strike support was not extensive and involved only a small minority. Whether discontent was native or immigrant was not apparent. At Polish Nanticoke all mineworkers quit on July 28 and returned just over two months later; no particular nationality appeared to stand out in the conflict. One Ukrainian historian wrote that operators did import pioneers of his nationality as scabs at this time, but if this was so, they were few in number, unnoticed, and certainly did not affect the outcome.[38]

Both disputes in the decade, then, revealed the recurrent drawbacks to unionization that can be seen to characterize the area to the end of the century. The inability to conduct a well-coordinated strategy in all three fields was a significant failing. Mineworkers of all districts were not able to synchronize their grievances to establish an inclusive association of maximum strength.

Another obstacle was an external one, the employer. The operators had joined and prepared for the Long Strike for some time. The indomitable Gowen and his

75

colleagues were adamant and held out until they had nearly annihilated the WBA. And two years later, while some companies eschewed wage cuts, the major Wyoming producers steadfastly persisted until their strikers, too, asked for mercy.

A third drawback to organizational success might be called labor leaders' conservatism. Siney particularly considered the enemy of the union to be overproduction, not the producer. He guided his organization toward cooperation with capital, not toward conflict. An aggressive union might have dominated the industry in the late 1860's and afterward, instead of sharing it with the many small operators. Certainly 1875 would have been fought on more equal terms, if at all. By 1877 the unions among the miners were small and insignificant, and extensive organizational efforts were fruitless.

The nationality hypothesis for strike failure is, then, inapplicable here. Before 1880 the East European composition of the anthracite districts was barely perceptible and, even when present in selected communities, did not destroy unionism or defeat strikes. Operators may well have imported single Slavs during the disturbances or larger numbers at other times. But these were merely the pioneers of a new ethnic strain. Even in the early 1880's most were lost among the American and West European colonies. An official of the Pennsylvania Department of Agriculture at the turn of the century expressed the situation most clearly:

Q. How many years have these Huns been in these mining districts? A. Twenty years ago you could

not find an Italian or a Hungarian. Those nationalities were scarce in the coal regions. The present
condition commenced, probably . . . since 1885,
1886, 1887 and 1888. There might have been a
few scattered before then. I doubt whether up to
1880 or 1882, two per cent of the miners were adult
Italians, Hungarians, or Polish . . . possibly up to
1884 or 1885.[39]

One would have to wait until the next period of unrest
in the hard-coal area, 1887–1888, to analyze again the
forces in the struggle and assess specifically East European reaction to labor conflict.

V

A Slavic Community Strikes

AS IN THE 1870'S, SO IN THE 1880'S, THE MINERS FAILED to establish a permanent labor organization. Additional obstacles this time were inadequate union direction and jealousy between two unions involved, the Knights of Labor and the Amalgamated Association of Miners and Mine Laborers. Yet the usually proffered explanation of failure is again East European demoralization of the union cause. The labor organizers could not reach the clannish Slavs ignorant of English. Communication with the immigrant before and during a strike was impossible, it is claimed, and the resulting confusion was calamitous for labor.

Contemporary observers unanimously pointed to the Slavs' presence in the 1887–1888 strike as the cause of labor failure. John R. Commons, for example, concluded: "The [union] defeat at this time is ascribed with una-

79

nimity to the presence of the cheap labor of southern [and eastern] Europe, which could not be controlled or organized according to the methods then pursued. The operators were able to play . . . one nationality against another nationality."[1] His view may have come from reporters covering the strike, one of whom related after it ended: "Nearly every officer of organized labor that I met expressed the fear that whenever they struck, the Poles and Hungarians and Italians were poured out to take their places."[2] Others, too, blamed the immigrant for weakening the men's resistance: "Anthracite operators welcomed the 'Slavs' because [they] could keep wages down and break striking as was done in 1887–1888."[3] Anthracite-area specialists observed: "The presence of this [Slavic] class of laborers no doubt contributed to the defeat of the strike of 1887–1888" and "These widely differing races [of Central Europe] broke down the miners' solidarity and made effective unionization of the coal fields impossible."[4]

Even recent analysts indict the East Europeans: in 1957 one student wrote: "One factor which undoubtedly contributed to the failure of the strike of 1887–1888 was the great change then going on in the character of the population of the anthracite region. . . . About 1880 . . . the United States witnessed the beginning of a mass immigration of Poles, Lithuanians, Hungarians, and Italians, and many of these people moved into the anthracite region."[5]

Yet, just as before, factors other than nationality hindered organization; a new problem of dual unionism was soon added to the old one of incomplete organization. The demographic change, that is, the entrance of the Slav, in fact actually strengthened the union cause rather than weakened it. A survey of the two unions involved and the events leading to the dispute will show determined Slavic support.

Prosperity quickly dispelled the hard times of 1877 and stimulated labor reformers to activity. Both Gowen and Parrish led employers in mollifying demands and in increasing salaries slightly in 1878 and 1879. But crumb-throwing did not satisfy a vigorous labor organization, the Knights of Labor, whose strength centered around their Scranton stronghold at this time. About 1879 one Knight, Chris Evans, led the Order into all coal districts, soft and hard, but the progress masked a deep split within the national body, one which would lead to labor's hated defect of "dualism." A second labor group, the Amalgamated Association of Miners and Mine Laborers, was to break off from the Knights and compete with them for members. This cancer of dualism was to sap union strength into the 1890's.

Two features of the Knights caused dissidents to form a competing labor association, their secret nature and their inclusion of all trades. Some miners objected to the secrecy, and they sought a trade union body of and for mineworkers. The Order reacted by establishing its own assembly of coal workers, District 135, but Evans himself started a separate national group in 1885. A contest for members in the fields ensued.

81

The two groups at the state level, the Knights and the Amalgamated Association of Miners and Mine Laborers of Pennsylvania, continually sought a modus vivendi, which was to break apart in crisis. The secret body had the larger membership. It expanded quickly into the middle coal field especially after 1885 when Catholic opposition to the group lessened. The conservative leadership of the other union, the Amalgamated, reminded old-timers of the WBA in its heyday. George Harris, the thirty-year-old AA president, did somewhat resemble Siney with his self-contained manner, staid appearance, and "earnest," though "not eloquent," speech.[6] The Englishman also had a labor philosophy much like that of the old WBA chief. As an anthracite-district paper described it, the Amalgamated "does not encourage strikes"; rather its aim was arbitration.[7]

But the conservatism of the union did not inhibit Harris' missionary fervor. He personally launched an organization drive in Schuylkill, the WBA's graveyard, and by 1885 achieved some success, especially around the old WBA headquarters in Pottsville. Other signs, such as a very large labor demonstration in Shenandoah, encouraged organizers, and by the fall of 1885 Harris had recruited fifteen thousand Schuylkill men and even some in Lehigh.

At this time worsening economic conditions and an industrywide wage cut stimulated newly confident members to demand vigorous Amalgamated retaliation in a strike. But characteristically Harris backed away from conflict, accepting the Reading's assurance of no further

82

reductions. In answer to the outraged cries of radicals, a wise miner reminded hotheads of that omnipresent union deficiency, an entirely unorganized field. He asked readers to recall the 1875 debacle when Wyoming was not with them, and inquired finally: "Men, will we 'leap again in the dark?' "[8]

Meanwhile, try as they might, neither the AA nor the Knights could enlist northerners outside the Knights' stronghold; perhaps Wyoming men still remembered southern apathy to their efforts in 1877. The relationship between the two unions, in their efforts to increase membership, varied during the next two years, as tension mounted and events led to an outbreak in September, 1887.

Until 1886 the Amalgamated had worked completely separately from the Knights. Each of the two groups sought to organize the workers under its own philosophy. But as the men became more "union conscious," a working arrangement became necessary to minimize rivalry in recruitment and present a common front to the operators. The Knights, the Amalgamated, and a third, small group, the Eccentric Engineers, agreed to meet periodically as a joint committee. The committee functioned into the 1887–1888 strike, but unfortunately this union association was never able to reconcile differences entirely and avoid friction. Dissension was to destroy them all.

At first the joint body appeared to be aggressive. It demanded better wages, hours, and working conditions through the first half of 1886. And in November the unions agreed to a more substantial "federation," supported by a per capita tax. But such determination had little substance. Few operators responded to the resolutions, and the Lehigh mineowners were especially adamant. Within the union association the old issues of secrecy and trade unionism still produced internal bickering, and news of union divisions broke into the papers. The sympathetic *News-Dealer,* for example, feared that the mutual spying going on would hurt both the Knights and the AA; it observed sadly, "The bitterest animosity is felt at the present time."[9]

The rank and file, however, were less concerned with labor jealousies; they clamored more for bread-and-butter improvements, and their representatives tried to respond. In January, 1887, a Knights meeting at Hazleton attempted to ratify a new wage demand. But the timidity of the Wyoming representatives, who recognized their own weakness, forced the conference to withdraw the proposal; and after the operators ignored two similar requests from the joint committee, the miners' group decided to postpone any retaliatory strike action until the fall.

The constantly recurring internal dissension might have in part caused the delay, for the rivalry for members continued. A "miner" answered a Knights' leader's boast that soon all the mineworkers would join the Order: "Whilst you have two [organizations in the anthracite district], you are a prey to capital; but [since] you are determined to have the two, you must also be prepared to suffer the consequences."[10] The consequences were to be serious.

During the summer of 1887 relations between workers and employers were coming to a head. The joint committee shelved its internal difficulties temporarily and in August demanded a higher pay raise than ever, 15 percent, or negotiation with all middle and southern operators. The response of employers was mixed. Only the Reading, then in receivership and financially insecure, agreed to a conference. The joint committee called out the men elsewhere, mainly in Lehigh, in an order to be effective September 10.

In the few days before the stoppage union officials must have endured considerable soul-searching. The two organizations had always tried to their utmost to avoid industrial warfare. Neither President Harris of the AA nor Powderly of the Knights ever advocated strikes, but now one was at hand, the first real test for both. The uncertainty over the contest and the attitude of the men may well have unsettled some leaders, but there had been some reassuring trends.

Both unions had added a good number of miners to their organizations. Four years of Harris' missionary work had accomplished a great deal; the Amalgamated believed that it could count on thirty thousand men in the two lower fields. The Knights there probably added ten thousand more to the union rolls. The Amalgamated throughout wanted to emulate the WBA's success in retaining workers' loyalty but hoped to avoid its failure, the 1875 debacle.

Now in 1887 new conditions forced the Amalgamated

85

to develop techniques additional to those of John Siney. A change had come over the territory in the 1880's, a factor Siney never had to deal with—the influx of the Slav. Both the AA and the Knights hoped that their relations with the forty-three thousand non-English-speaking immigrants would prove favorable in this ordeal. They could not be sure, however, since neither had emphasized the attraction of aliens. The fact is that the attitude of both unions toward the Slav in the early eighties had really been ambivalent. The approach of the Amalgamated was typical. On one hand, it utilized foreign-language speakers to win immigrant loyalty at nationality rallies; but, on the other hand, organizers at English-speaking meetings railed against the Hungarians for tearing down American standards.

At the big Shenandoah rally in April, 1885, a Captain Jeniski "addressed the Poles and Hungarians in their own language," after which six AA locals were formed.[11] The union also conceded to Jeniski's request to have the Amalgamated's bylaws printed in Polish.

The organization did not entirely ignore those foreigners in its Wyoming drive, either. The union employed one Frank Akson, an "intelligent Pole," to harangue his people at Plymouth and Mill Creek, and organizers even established a Polish branch of the AA.[12] Yet at the same time Harris and other Association officials condemned the evils of immigrant labor introduced into the region to work at starvation rates.

Before 1887 the Knights of Labor also generally neglected to follow a firm policy toward the newcomers from East Europe. Powderly personally was sympathetic to the plight of the Slavs and even hoped that they might join his organization in a body.[13] And on occasion the Order did try to win their support. In fact, the most prominent anthracite-region Ukrainian, Father Wolansky, headed a Knights-sponsored assembly at Shenandoah. But English-speaking locals also described them as inferiors, and on the whole the Knights' attempts to reach the Bohemians, Poles, and Italians were not highly successful. The aliens, too, did not appear especially hospitable. Aside from the language difficulty, the general suspicion of the Catholic Church may have discouraged the Slav from joining such a society.

Thus, union-Slav relations in the years until 1887 were tenuous and vacillating. Few immigrants were dues-paying members; the two major labor organizations in the anthracite districts primarily represented English-speaking groups. The Amalgamated drew the English, Welsh, and German mineworkers, probably the highly skilled workers, while most of the Knights were Irish.

So with the strike call in early September the joint committee apprehensively watched the reaction of Lehigh's five thousand immigrant mineworkers. The agreeable news of about nine thousand workers out on the first day soothed their anxiety. By September 13 the number had swelled to about thirty thousand, half of them in the Lehigh field. The rest who quit lived around Shamokin and in Schuylkill, for southern independent mineowners had also refused any increase. Union power, so long dormant, had again stung Coxe Brothers, Lehigh Coal and Navigation, the Pardees, Markle, Lehigh Valley, and the small operators.

The men were jubilant. "The order to strike was obeyed implicitly by the men, and not one remained at work other than the pumpmen and engineers who were permitted to continue by the committee's instructions." In the middle district "not a drill or pick is used nor a pound of coal mined."[14] The Lehigh nationalities had held together.

However, the strike chiefs had to win the fight, not just start one. First, the joint committee had to complete negotiations with the Reading. At a conference the two sides agreed to a compromise, a temporary 8 percent raise until January 1, when the Reading could pay whatever the struck operators then offered the others. Some Shamokin and Mt. Carmel producers fell in line behind their competitor and thus confined the battleground to the middle region alone.

The joint committee also set up a relief system and funneled contributions from the now better-paid southerners to their idle compatriots. It appealed also to the Knights working on the Reading Railroad to boycott any scab coal shipped from Lehigh and to contribute money. These employees so resolved at a mid-October convention and asked Powderly for national aid. A state meeting of Knights added help, and other gifts may have come from more distant points. The distributions at their height reached about seven thousand dollars per week. The strike leaders now awaited the capitulation of the Lehigh independents.

But these entrepreneurs were made of stern stuff. Immediately after the strike call E. B. Coxe told those employees who quit to collect their pay and clear out of their company homes. Ario Pardee still opposed any conference with outside agitators who, he said, interfered with his relations with his men. The walkout must have particularly irritated John Markle. After a three-months' strike in 1885 he and his employees had agreed to submit future differences to their own arbitration board. But now, two years later, outsiders were asking his men to repudiate that arrangement.

The Lehigh producers tried to break the strike in November by offering a 4½ percent increase to anyone who would return. But the men stayed away. The winter drew on, and labor's optimism changed to grim determination. Christmas for the strikers was a sad one.

The new year brought new complications to the Lehigh stalemate. The conflict spread to the Schuylkill field by way of the Reading's nonmining employees. The railroad workers, members of a Knight's assembly, had grievances of their own: the firing of some Knights in 1886, the institution of an eye test in 1887, and the Reading's handling of scab Lehigh coal during the entire fall. Suspicion of a secret pact between the Philadelphia and Reading (P and R) and the middle-field coal operators added to the railroaders' dissatisfaction. Finally, after the Reading discharged some freight crews for refusing to load coal, the local Knights' assembly on December 28 called out every employee in the railroad system.

Undoubtedly the plight of Lehigh mineworkers and the Reading freight employees affected the P and R coal miners deeply. In fact a handful of Reading mine-workers had already walked out in sympathy. So when the Schuylkill operator announced in late December the removal of the 8 percent raise according to the September arrangement, the workers heatedly objected. The joint committee requested a conference, but the Reading was adamant. The union group had no alternative but to call a strike for January 1 against the Reading and other operators who had returned to the old pay scale. Engineers and other maintenance men were permitted to remain at work everywhere, and locals were allowed to decide on their own whether to go out where the raise had been continued.

The results of this new call encouraged the leaders, just as they had in September. On January 3, forty-nine of the Reading's fifty-three collieries had to shut down, and the remaining twenty-five of twenty-eight independents working were still paying the 8 percent. By mid-January the number of operating mines was reduced to only a few in the entire field. Optimism again filled the committee's Pottsville headquarters. One-half of the entire anthracite work force was idle. W. T. Lewis, master workman of the Knights' miners' Assembly 135, arrived to assume leadership of the now bidistrict struggle.

But the large following hid certain profound weaknesses and misunderstandings. First, the Knights themselves were in disagreement. Their General Executive Board did not approve of the railroaders' walkout or formally endorse either work stoppage until February 7. Second, allowing locals the strike decision where the raise was continued made for rank-and-file confusion, bewilderment, and dissatisfaction. The joint committee itself and large collieries receiving the 8 percent were badly split over the issue. A third problem was the division among the Knights' railroad men, mineworkers in the Order, and members of the Amalgamated. The conflict of these three distinct interests did not appear until the end of the strike itself.

Actually the stoppage ended rather quickly, especially in the south. By early February the Reading claimed the return of many disillusioned strikers. Rather suddenly in the middle of the month the miners' general, Lewis, conferred with Powderly. He then called the Schuylkill workers back to their positions at company terms by the twentieth. While surprised and disgusted at Lewis' hasty surrender, local assemblies did comply. However, some were so unnerved that they returned their founding charters.

From that point the outcome in the two other battles was a matter of time. The Reading railroad men and the Lehigh mineworkers yielded a few weeks later; they both asked for peace by mid-March. Except for the Scranton citadel and a few smaller labor bastions, anthracite-area unionism had once more been destroyed. Long after the public lost interest came the bitter fruit of defeat, an appeal for the starving families of seven hundred blacklisted strike leaders.[15]

It was in the last month of the struggle that Lewis' reason for his stunning capitulation—the internal stress

91

of component factions—became clear. In essence it was the traditional split between the Amalgamated's trade unionism and the Knights of Labor "all-for-one" policy. The most active Knights' representative in the affair was the railroaders' head, John L. Lee. His activities particularly antagonized the Amalgamated man on the committee and even some mineworker members of the Order. From the start in late December, in true Knights' fashion, he sought to tie the trainmen's strike to the mineworkers' quest for better pay. On the last day of 1887, for example, he insisted that the mineworkers' issue was not merely wages and hours but, more basically, fraternity: "The miners are going to stand by their [railroad] brethren in the fight for organized labor."[16] This view Lee held to the end. Thus when Lewis surrendered, Lee fumed that the railroaders were left to fend for themselves. But Lewis knew of the increasing dissatisfaction among the Amalgamated representatives, who regarded Lee's statements as distortions.

The AA officials were more conservative and had had a different impression of the strike all along. Even at the start Amalgamated leaders had agreed reluctantly to the walkout. After it began, they regarded the issue as one of miner interests alone, certainly not support of the railway men. In a lengthy interview, just prior to the Reading mineworkers' strike, Mr. Anthony Lally, president of the AA's Ashland branch, expressed his organization's caution toward any stoppage and associating with the trainmen. Asked if a strike at that time would be unwise, this widely respected "most levelheaded" miner observed: "Well, yes. No good results ever come from strikes. I am opposed to anything of the kind. If the men were to strike and remain idle one month it would take five months to recover the loss thus sustained with the eight percent increase granted." He reminded his listener of painful memories: "We had a six months' strike in 1874 [sic]. The miners in this region were forced to seek employment elsewhere, and most of them went to Luzerne and other coal fields. The strike was a terrible blow to this county. It paralyzed business, and when the end came out people discovered they were holding the cow by the horns while the Luzerne operators and miners were doing the milking." And again, "The lessons of past strikes have demonstrated the folly of such action." The reporter asked Lally about the miners' relations with the railroaders: "It is said . . . that the miners are in sympathy with the striking railroad men and will go out if ordered." Lally's answer came quickly: "I don't believe our men will strike on a pretext of that kind. Sympathy is cheap, but when you talk of strikes it involves dollars and cents and that touches a tender spot."[17]

Later Amalgamated action continued to reject Lee's unity hypothesis. In a formal statement the AA's executive board, some Knights, and the joint committee announced in late January: "Of this railroad matter we have little or nothing to say, for that is not or has not been made by anyone with authority to speak for the miners an issue of their strike."[18] Elsewhere, too, the Amalgamated branches rejected the Knights' attempt to tie the dispute of miner and railroader in one protest.

The AA local at Shenandoah's William Penn Mine continually seemed more willing to return because they were "outspoken in condemnation of the effort to keep them idle on the railroad issue."[19]

Poor strike direction and internal conflict led to distress among the rank and file looking for strong leadership. Allowing some to work while friends were idle particularly confused and dissatisfied the ordinary mineworker. One old laborer of Mahanoy City commented: "With wise and intelligent leaders the miners' strike could have been avoided. . . . The joint committee called me out on a strike. And for what? Why [sic] to stop the company from marketing the product of my labor, and at the same time they will allow my brother miners, working for the other companies, to work day and night to make up my quota in the market. Is this unity?"[20] A local newspaper also could not understand why the unions allowed high-wage coal to be shipped over all railroads, including the Reading. A former labor leader said that the union chiefs were out of touch with their members' feelings and should have separated the complicating railroad trouble from the first issue.[21]

Still another factor contributed to failure: the unaffected Wyoming field. Both organizations had tried with little success to recruit members in this most productive anthracite region before the dispute broke out. Despite the contest going on to the south, the northern men carried their lunch pails to work every day. To be sure, in two actions they did express their sympathies, first by financial contributions and later by making demands on

94

their own employers. But the resolution lacked conviction, for when the Wyoming companies refused their demands, they took no action. One reporter offered two reasons for the northerners' timidity: the grievances were not serious enough and "the old miners," the ones who perhaps recalled 1877, "were opposed to [any] movement."[22] A Schuylkill delegation exhorting them to action returned home without any commitment.

And what about the "Hungarians," that new society which had already begun to crowd into the anthracite districts and which the labor unions had cursed, yet cajoled? Did they ignore the summons for the walkout? Were they the first to return to work? The answers are all in the negative. If it was in any way effective, their behavior, part of the structure of their community, stiffened strike resistance.

Of course not all, not even most, of the Slavs were labor crusaders. They merely followed the mineworking majority. In Wyoming, for example, the ten thousand foreigners remained on the job with their twenty thousand English-speaking neighbors.[23] In the two southern areas the response of all the mineworkers satisfied the joint committee.

The first distinctively ethnic activity was a massive exodus of immigrants from the industry looking for employment. In both affected regions newspapers dwelled on their outward movement to get work. In Lehigh the number of "hunkies" who left ran into the thousands a fortnight after the strike began, including an entire settle-

95

ment of five hundred known as Slabtown. Almost all the Hazleton Lithuanians left at that time. A more noticeable exodus took place in Schuylkill when that area struck. One observer asserted that the foreigners were "leaving the country in droves. . . . 'Huns' cannot bear to be idle and they are leaving to work elsewhere."[24] Still another condemned the stench about the train depot which the foreigners had brought from their hovels. A nativist welcomed their departure in a good-riddance-to-bad-rubbish manner. But he offered an important addition: "The exodus of Huns is hailed with delight by all classes, although they are heartily in sympathy with the strikers."[25] Thus a good many, rather than remaining on relief in the field, left for jobs elsewhere, going to the Old World, out West, or to the Wyoming district. But withal they sympathized with the cause.

Of course not all Slavs moved, so the query as to their behavior in the area remains: Did they return to the mines early? Or did their greenhorn relatives rush in and kill the strike as alleged? With some exceptions, the findings remain negative. Certain features of the industry prohibited the use of inexperienced hands. Introducing new workers into the anthracite industry by operators would on this account be risky. Some occupations required experience, particularly the underground work in which explosives were handled. For that reason mineowners hesitated importing new men during a dispute. The Reading, for example, brought in far fewer mineworkers than it did railroad men. Thus, most of the work that did continue throughout was above ground, such as running culm through breakers, and therefore unimportant.

A review of early attempts at the resumption of work in general proves that East Europeans rarely sided with the mineowner. In fact when the immigrants did act, they did so as a community in spontaneous, grass-roots violence which dumbfounded the entire anthracite-region population. These outbreaks demonstrated the nature of their allegiance to the labor standard, an allegiance for cause rather than merely to the unions per se. It was true that individual East Europeans did continue on the job during the conflict, but these were unrepresentative of their group. A large number whom employers, the Reading especially, did recruit were American farmhands from the surrounding countryside, willingly engaged for off-season income. The Lehigh Coal Company tried to entice a group of Belgian miners just landing at New York, but the attempt was unsuccessful. The only successful immigrant importation was a carload of Italians taken to Mahanoy City to work on the railroad, not in the mines.

Significant incidents of unrest revealed East European hostility toward the mineowner and those newly hired. For the perspicacious a small strike in Wyoming just before the conflict signaled Slavic reaction. It was a preview of immigrant belligerency and fearlessness toward apparent operator abuse. The scene was the Alden Coal Company just below Wilkes-Barre; the major protagonist was an exacting foreman.

About the middle of July a docking boss, Thomas

97

Cavanaugh, fired some mineworkers who objected to his excessive deductions in their pay. The company then hired some new men led by one Jack Hooley and Michael Christ. Among these recruits were newly arrived Slavic immigrants. For three weeks the dispossessed workers pressured the novices to leave by threatening them with poison, assassination, and starvation.

In the evening of August 8 the desperate strikers acted. As soon as the workers appeared at the mine head and prepared to leave, violence broke out. "The strikers assailed their enemies with clubs, stones, and pistols, and beat some of them in a terrible manner."[26] The assault was definitely a group affair, as women also participated. Their nationality was obvious from a banner held aloft proclaiming in Polish, "Kill the men who have taken the bread out of our mouths."[27] The strikers, armed with fence paling, ran "like wild Indians" after the workers who fled across the adjacent field. When caught, twelve of the greenhorns dropped to the ground senseless under the blows of their pursuers. Some lucky ones were able to crawl home. After the melee a hundred guards were posted to protect the remainder of the men willing to work.

Hooley was attacked the next day on his way home. Asssailants jumped out of the bush and mauled him "until he was used up and begged for mercy."[28] Authorities held Andrew Shillock, Andrew Nowak, John Ponorski, Thomas Viczik, and John Brantz for leading the attacks. Of course the arrest of these men does not indicate their guilt, but it certainly aids in determining the nationality involved.

Christ evaded the strikers' fury, but Cavanaugh, the boss, was not so fortunate. Like Hooley, walking home on the evening of the twenty-fourth, he "was brutally assaulted . . . by three Polanders. . . . His cries for mercy seemed to have no effect on his assailants. . . . It is stated . . . he received several ugly scalp wounds, that his arm was broken and that his face was battered to a jelly."[29] The so-called pauper labor had broadcast its grievance.

This kind of expression occurred again in the major dispute which began in Lehigh the next month. Pardee initiated the discontent by introducing about one hundred Italians to work his Hollywood strippings in mid-September. But striking countrymen had gotten to them, for only fourteen showed up for roll call. Even at these few "their fellows were furious. They armed themselves with bludgeons and the ubiquitous stilettos and started out for vengeance. The union men had hard work to hold them back. 'Wc kill-a them!' They cried fiercely, 'No black-a-leg us!' But the strikers held them back. What arguments they used with the obdurate fourteen is not known, but yesterday no one showed his face at the mine."[30]

This minor unrest in the middle field really did not attract much notice. In general the public commended both sides for the pacific nature of the dispute. "The quiet demeanor of the men out on strike is a subject of general remark. Not only is this the case here at home, but from all parts of the region come similar reports."[31] Slavic and Anglo-Saxon mineworkers appeared calmly determined and according to one account passed the time playing cards. A shooting, then, in Shenandoah came as a rude shock.

Shenandoah then was a thriving community. Second in size in the county to Pottsville, it sat in a small valley on some of the richest coal veins in the district. In the two decades before 1888 it had grown about six times to fourteen thousand, of which a quarter were Slavs. Shenandoah more than any other community in the 1880's had attracted Poles, Lithuanians, Ukrainians, and Slovaks in search of work. Many lived in the "Rocks" section, an area the nicer element avoided. The atmosphere of the ghetto, a cluster of immigrant boardinghouses, was unpleasant, as offensive odors emitted from manure heaps, garbage, ash piles, and coal mud.[32]

When the strike began, Knights of Labor officials altered their usual distant relations with Slavs by urging Shenandoah immigrants to join. The union employed a Polish organizer to recruit among his kind. His success was to be not so much increased membership but rather stronger enthusiasm for the strikers' cause. The Slavic temper rose when the Reading began to open some workings in January. The confusing union policy of allowing some, but not others, to work had bewildered the Shenandoah Slavs as much as other mineworkers, but the immigrant uncertainty turned to collective aggression when a handful of Slavs began to scab. The viciousness of the assaults on these individuals stunned even the strike leaders themselves.

The incidents began on February 1. Unknown attackers clubbed eleven Hungarians working at the Suffolk colliery. Union officials immediately deprecated the attack. On the same day seventy-five women tried to persuade nonunion men to quit the Glendower Mine and offered them loaves of bread. When the workers refused and hurried off to their trolley, they were pursued by the infuriated females, shouting epithets and hurling the bread after them. The superintendent's testimony and newspaper accounts strongly indicate the Slavic nationality of these assailants in both these disturbances.[33]

The next morning heavier missiles flew. About a score of foreigners headed toward the William Penn Mine, which the union had allowed to operate. But on the way some young men stoned them, "seized their dinner kettles, threw away the contents, threatened to kill them and drove them back to their shanties."[34] The uneasy operators increased the number of their protectors, the coal-and-iron police. Blood ran on Friday, February 3.

As the workday ended, the Shenandoah City Mine, where fifty East Europeans had been working, attracted a crowd of eight hundred Polish strikers. As the workers began to leave, the indignant Slavs showered them with rocks, coal, and snowballs. Hearing the commotion, four coal-and-iron policemen rushed to assist those assaulted. Officers Moyer and Diebert arrested one Pole for stoning, and Officers Shane and Krieger another. Then when the guards began using their gun butts to clear away the crowd, a group of about fifty foreigners tore off fence paling, charged the police, and wrestled away one of the prisoners. They knocked down and frisked Diebert while another "Hun busied himself belaboring Moyer with a

101

board."[35] Moyer on the ground meanwhile fired his pistol at his assailants in self-defense. After the smoke had cleared and the crowd had scattered, six people lay wounded: two bystanders and four Polish strikers. During the melee policeman Krieger had escaped with his man, Joseph Wasilowski.

Krieger fled to Squire Shoemaker's and arrived not much before a crowd of five hundred, who, crying for the prisoner, began to hurl missiles through windows. The aroused mob then pulled off an iron railing and used it to beat down the door. The Squire, judging appeasement healthier than valor, quickly released the Pole on bail and sent him out to his friends. "The crowd, elated with their victory, wildly cheered the prisoner and rushed him off."[36]

At the same time local authorities had arrested Moyer and Diebert for the shooting and spirited them away to another office, Squire Monaghan's. This gentleman took the precaution of barricading the door after the coal-and-iron police captain, David Christian, had arrived. Again, "The mob outside had meanwhile become larger and more unruly with its Polish elements."[37] As stones began crashing through windows, the prisoners begged to be incarcerated. The climax occurred when one Joseph Schwincuffski was let in to place assault and battery charges against the two. By this time the crowd was out of control. They pulled down an entire side of the house in a few minutes. Squire Monaghan advised the men to jump out a rear window to a trap door ten feet below and make their way to the stationhouse. They hastily complied while the one-legged Irish town official and a police friend went out to quiet the mob.

Officer Reilly admonished the crowd from the doorway and "stepped aside just in time to allow the Squire to stop a well-directed missile. Monaghan gasped for breath. . . . The Squire, his celtic blood aroused, ran out the door, grasped the big Hun, who had hit him, and belabored him right and left, finishing up with a blow from his wooden leg, the [Hun] being quite disabled by a blow on the shin."[38]

Of course this scuffle further agitated the crowd. Several jumped on the Squire and pummeled him until he collapsed. Finally Burgess Boehm and Sheriff Duffy arrived with a posse, dispersed the mob, and took the precaution of closing the saloons.

But order did not return, as the foreigners continued to vent their anger. At the Kohinoor Mine some other Poles assaulted workingmen, and "a Polander" shot a foreman. But enough citizens of other nationalities stepped into the fray to restore order.

Another near tragedy occurred not far from the Lehigh Valley station. John Radsworth, having worked at Park Place colliery, alighted from the trolley and went to see where the commotion came from. "Being in his working clothes, the Poles took him for a 'scab' and went for him. He hit a fellow a resounding whack in the face with his dinner can and another with his fist." But finding himself outnumbered, he withdrew, "carrying away some bad bruises." A local grocer, Mike Graham, tried to pacify the crowd but had to hide from a volley of stones. "The

Poles amused themselves . . . taking their aim on him," but nothing serious resulted.[39] Peace came by nine in the evening. But while the weary townspeople hoped that the rioting had spent itself, other working collieries continued to inflame the immigrants on Saturday.

In an open field just south of the active Kehley Run colliery a group began to form in midafternoon. Just before the four o'clock whistle the gathering had grown to a crowd of thousands. Five hundred or more determined Poles "were in the front rank," while the English-speaking spectators looked on expectantly.[40]

Captain Christian meanwhile had led a score of coal-and-iron guards to the mine to escort the workers home. The tension mounted until the impatient breaker boys broke away from their protectors. A dozen men pounced on the youths and began clouting them with the omnipresent fence palings. Other foreigners hurled stones and ice at the adult workers and their guards. Christian's men, however, rallied, stood their ground, and protected their charges' escape. The police then retreated slowly toward their headquarters at Indian Ridge Mine. The mob followed and threw missiles. One "Polander fired [at] Oscar Witman, a Pottsville member of the coal and iron men, [who] fell with a bullet through . . . one of his thighs."[41] Christian ordered his men to shoot, and when the firing ceased, six Poles lay wounded, though none seriously. The stunned mob drew back long enough for the coal-and-iron policemen to escape to their quarters, a converted railroad train. Some rioters regrouped later, to hang around the cars. They finally dispersed when Christian received five more groups of reinforcements, about three hundred men in all.

Thus it was not until the evening that the authorities could effectively control events. The foreigners had said their piece forcefully: "The rioting Poles . . . do not propose to allow anybody [to] work . . . and insist that what they do is . . . to maintain a solid strike, and [it] will be adhered to."[42] Both the union leadership and even Slavic leaders themselves criticized the outbreaks severely.

The continued violence frightened the conservative joint committee, which abhorred antagonizing public opinion. The labor generals early disavowed any responsibility. According to one newspaper "Strike leaders such as Lee, [Secretary] Duffy, [President] Davis [of the Amalgamated], et al., deprecate riots and say 'twas the work of ignorant foreigners and worthless outsiders who do not belong to labor organizations."[43] Another reported, "The labor leaders say the riot of a few Poles has nothing to do with the strike."[44] Throughout the strike the labor leaders begged for peace.

Just after the mobs had stoned the citizens' homes on Friday, Lee and Duffy counseled moderation at a public meeting in Robbins' Opera House. Word of Saturday's approaching violence also distressed them. Later, at a Knights' advisory board meeting, two Poles were sent out to persuade the crowd to disperse. But the pleas of these countrymen, a Girardville Knight and a local district attorney, went unheeded.

According to a report in the *Philadelphia Record,*

while the battle raged at Kehley Run, the board members even asked to be sworn into Burgess Boehm's posse to try reasoning with the foreigners. Here they were successful at last, although only after the shooting. "The angry Poles dispersed and went muttering to their shanties."[45]

Another evening meeting at Robbins' Opera House heard more labor leaders beg for peace. A national organizer of the Knights directed his remarks to prominent Poles: "Remember your pledge and obey the law." The union sent out a similar appeal in a multilanguage circular and asked Slavic priests to caution their congregations.

Catholic religious leaders readily complied.[46] In fact, with the exception of the Ukrainian Father Wolansky, they had had no sympathy for the strikers. The Polish cleric, Father Lenarkiewicz, particularly condemned the violence. In the midst of the Saturday riot he went through the streets with the authorities and urged that the mobs disperse. And throughout the struggle his sermons demanded that his listeners return to work. On the other hand, the Greek Catholic leader, Father Wolansky, was singular in his support of the strike.

Whatever the Church's position was in the strike, the truest and most significant expression of East European feeling toward the riots came on Monday evening at a rally called by Father Wolansky. Here in the jammed Opera House all the constituent nationalities had articulate representatives on stage: the editors Szlupas of the Lithuanian *Balsas* and Semenovich of the Ukrainian

106

Amerika, the Polish shoemaker Smoczynski, and the Slovak merchant Wislosky. Charley Rice, "headman of the foreigners for twenty years," led the meeting and after a ninety-minute session pronounced the resolutions.[47]

In action that was as dramatic as it was revealing, the Slavs accepted the responsibility for the violence. They took a position which went far to verify the stories in the local press. Yet while they assumed the onus of agitation, they also assumed its honor. As two newspapers explained, "The Polanders are . . . indignant at the whole responsibility of the riots. . . . They were [at] the front only because their abettors were too cowardly" and "The rioters have realized the folly of their action and feel a little sore because no English-speaking miners took part in the riots."[48]

So the immigrant admitted his actions and defied not only his union and his religious leaders but also the more weak-kneed Anglo-Saxon. It was largely the English workers who helped break up the riots on Friday and Saturday, and it was one of these whom a reporter overheard remarking: "Well, the Pole is right, and I'm wid 'em. If they'd got licked today I'd a helped 'em!"[49] The majority of the English- and German-speaking miners wanted to go to work, and it was the "'Merica miners" whom a Slav had condemned because they "sit at home and make bullets for the Polanders to fire" or the "'Merica men who sit idle and allow themselves to be cowed by the authorities."[50] And as "one of the lessons of the present strike," it was the "quiet and peaceable . . . native American" whom another observer compared

107

The Slavic Community on Strike

to the "foreign born laborer who seized every chance to foment strife and indulge in violences."[51]

That the 1887–1888 dispute again temporarily crushed anthracite-region unionism is the event's obvious lesson. But rather than the influx of Old World peasants, other, recurrent factors caused the disaster: a divided union leadership with ambiguous strike tactics, an entire coal district operating throughout the strike, resolute mineowners, and perhaps a lukewarm Anglo-Saxon population. The Hungarian's contribution to the struggle was in support of the cause and stemmed from his motive for immigrating, "za chlebem."

Some on that quest for bread immediately left the coal region for other money-making locations or to return to Europe. Recently arrived and mostly single, they were still highly mobile. Whether or not they moved, one could surmise that their ability to earn and save continued, even though they were now operating on a reduced income.

Undoubtedly the majority in the Slavic patch were in favor of the strike to assure a pay raise for all. And because of determined community sentiment, working dissenters had to pay for their transgressions. Here was the cause of the Slav-inspired beatings and riots. In this crisis the tightly knit East European society could not tolerate individualists. As one reporter put it: "The striking Poles and Huns mean to stop . . . work even if it leeds [sic] to murdering their own kinsmen. . . . They declare all Huns and Poles must stand together, live together, or fall and die together."[52]

108

A Slavic Community Strikes

That the major riot took place in Shenandoah, the most mature of the Slavic communities, was more than coincidence. Here strike loyalty approached fanaticism. On the other hand, the English-speaking miners, whether labor leaders or only followers, seemed less unified, more individualistic, less provident, and perhaps less determined.

The 1888 strike was the first time that the Slavic anthracite community participated as a whole in a labor dispute. Most "pauper labor" at this date were sophisticated enough to understand the implications of striking and, once agreed on quitting work, they literally fought for their rights at the work place. Even before the dispute began, an acute observer predicted the new immigrant behavior in terms of their endurance and their conformist attitude in labor disputes:

> It is almost ludicrous to hear them talk about the possibility of "foreign labor" being brought in, considering that they themselves are the so-called "foreign labor!" "Don't let them try it," they say boldly. "If they do, there will be bloodshed here. That's all there is about it." They have not been long in America, but they have been here long enough to learn that they are working for children's wages, and they are willing to fight for more. As a prominent Knight said, summing up the position of the better class of foreign speaking labor in the Lehigh region: "These men can stand out two weeks to the one week of English speaking miners. If we stand alone for three months, they are good for six. They can live on almost nothing. As for their spirit, they are full of it; and if it comes to fighting, you will find them in

the front ranks. I tell you it will not be healthy for the operators to try and import labor for settling up this question."[53]

The Slavs were found in the front ranks of the demonstrators, and they sacrificed much for labor victory. The divided unions unfortunately still did not recognize their contribution, and labor organization was now weakened for the reasons cited. Union sympathizers would have to wait another decade for the resurrection of labor power in the anthracite districts. Meanwhile other mineworkers sought the remedy to their ills in directly combating the immigrant menace.

VI

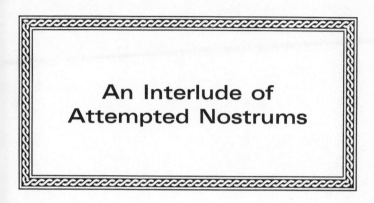

An Interlude of Attempted Nostrums

THE STRIKE OF 1887–1888 MAY HAVE DISCOURAGED the rank and file, but unionism as an idea dies hard. The more active workers could not accept a situation in which the operators completely controlled working conditions. Even if mineowners did improve wages and lower hours, their reforms might be only temporary, to be withdrawn without recourse for the worker. The basic grievances remained: low wages, excessive docking, no semi-monthly pay, and such; and as long as these ills existed, determined mineworkers would combat them.

In the next decade, the 1890's, labor organizers used two weapons. The first was the traditional, economic one of building a districtwide, or more hopefully an industrywide, union. The other was political. Labor leaders began to believe that with the mounting Slavic

111

influx, the poorer-paid East European was in fact preventing higher wages for Americans and Anglo-Saxons. Observing the junk heap of shanties at one end of town, the non-Slavic mineworker came to consider the new element therein as the major influence limiting his income. He might now agree with national labor leaders like Powderly and Gompers that the solution was more restrictive immigration legislation.

In the 1890's Pennsylvania did pass laws to limit the Slavic flow into the anthracite districts, but the older nationalities complained of their ineffectiveness. And unions continued to be weak or entirely absent, a condition frustrating labor sympathizers. Reformers could salvage some consolation. By 1897 a new labor missionary had arrived, an Irishman named John Fahy, who raised hopes that complete organization was at hand.

Union-building efforts after the 1888 strike were pathetic. In 1889 the Knights asked mineworkers' organizations to send delegates to a Wilkes-Barre conference, but the meeting accomplished nothing. The entire district seemed pessimistic and lacked enthusiasm for the union cause. The *Daily News-Dealer* had to apologize specifically for a Nanticoke reception at which labor "visitors were received very shabbily."[1]

Still, the reformers persisted and called a meeting again in 1890, this time in Schuylkill. In late March thirty-three delegates, representing fifteen thousand Schuylkill workers, met in the old WBA and AA headquarters in Pottsville. This session was as depressing as

112

the last. A *Public Ledger* reporter sympathized with most of the delegates, who, fearing blacklisting, refused to give interviews. He also noted the absence of any Wyoming and Hazleton representatives, although some did send sympathetic letters to the convention. The meeting resulted in the establishment of a Workingmen's Benevolent and Protective Association of the Anthracite Region, which soon disappeared.

Other leaders concentrated on a different solution to the mineworkers' problem: restricting the newer nationalities from the labor supply. All during the nineteenth century the anthracite industry, like other basic industries, received its manpower from the incoming immigrants. In the early days, during the 1820's and 1830's, the skilled English, Scotch, and Welsh entered and brought their experience from the British pits. Later incoming ethnic groups, first the Irish and later the Slavs, encountered resistance. The British-Irish conflict dissolved as both joined to criticize the East European as ignorant, accident prone, wage debasing, and a scab.

Protest arose in the eighties, particularly against the Slavic clannishness, drunkenness, ignorance of English, and general animal-like existence. The most articulate Americans sneered at their Sabbath revelry in saloons, where

> you will find the worst specimens of humanity to be found anywhere in the world. The habitués of these resorts are the off-scourings of Europe—brigands of the Carpathian Mountains, and the murderers of rural Hungary and the Russian steppes. The

113

men who constitute the choice convivial spirits of these murky, smoke-colored rooms are no farther along in human progress than were their ancestors, the hordes of Attila, when he led them howling up to the gates of Rome. These grimy saloons . . . present little pictures of a life that is not of this age. . . . They carry you back into the Burgundian taverns of the fourteenth century, into the bandits' dens of Upper Hungary.[2]

Another source of anti-Slavic criticism was the manner by which some were introduced into the region. Especially in the mid-1880's *John Swinton's Paper* exposed labor agents who on occasion did bring in groups of East Europeans.[3] In single incidents Anglo-Saxon workers even rioted against such importations.

Some blamed the immigrants for being chronically unsafe workers, characteristically reckless in the mines. Their desperate wish to earn money, one expert pointed out, forced them to neglect ordinary precautions and contribute to the high accident rate. For safety's sake, it was claimed, ethnic limitations were essential.[4]

The demographic shift itself in the anthracite region increased the bitterness against the Slav. The older nationalities alarmingly watched their numerical advantage shrink with the turn of the century. English-speaking workers leaving exceeded by far those arriving. With the unfavorable union climate after strikes, many of the better Anglo-Saxon workers, perhaps blacklisted or simply disillusioned, left the district for the western bituminous fields. A few others rose to supervisory positions in the companies. The alien multitude meanwhile filled the gaps. So it well might seem to hard-coal Americans that the lower-class "hunky" was expelling the Anglo-Saxon community. Such a shift had to be retarded.

A national nativist organization of the day added its weight to stopping the Hun inundation. This anti-Catholic and anti-immigrant body, the American Protective Association, had considerable influence in Pennsylvania in the 1890's and while prominent only in one area of the state, it did promote restrictionist legislation.[5] Thus with the disappearance of labor organization, immigration restriction through legislation became more popular. About 1889 the English-speaking population of the region, particularly Irish-Americans, sent many anti-Slavic petitions to Harrisburg. A representative, P. F. Caffrey, a mineworker himself from Ashley, below Nanticoke, responded by introducing a bill in April, 1889. The sponsors of the measure clothed the discrimination in a certification test for anthracite miners. For that position all candidates had to have two years' experience below ground and answer twelve questions *in English*. Any operator employing noncertified miners could be given a stiff fine. The bill passed easily.[6]

While the law should have barred East European job advancement and limited their numbers, its actual effect was nil. Indeed, few really wanted to enforce or obey the statute, for miners had reason to welcome the hard-working Slavic helpers. A prominent Irishman and a Welshman explained the miners' sentiments when one anti-immigrant petition was circulating through the coal fields. The first reminded his co-workers that the miners

115

themselves in their capacity as employers were attracting the foreigners. "It is all nonsense to say," he pointed out, "that the Hungarians are hurting anybody. . . . Irish and Welsh emigrants began to quit the area [about 1880] on the advice of friends." He concluded: "These people used to work in the mines as laborers, but as they do not come here any more [sic], the Hungarians fill the bill. . . . We hire their labor and are glad to get it." The Welshman not only agreed but added that the petitions really originated in the bituminous districts, and few anthracite-district workmen had wanted such legislation.[7] Even after the passage of the 1889 measure State Mine Inspector Williams told the "secret" of how the Slavs entered: "It is the miners [who] complain that are to blame for it. Many more than half . . . prefer Huns and Poles for laborers. . . . He [the miner] finds that he can get more work out of a Hun than he can out of one of his own class."[8]

Of course the operators and their supervisory assistants also welcomed the willing hands. Either as an excuse or as fact, they too claimed that without the Slavs' assistance there just would not be enough laborers, since Americans refused to do that sort of work.

While the Slavs continued to take the more menial positions, they were certainly not tools to be exploited at will. In their quest for bread they quickly grew dissatisfied with crusts. Miners of the mid-1880's attested to the new immigrants' uncanny knowledge of the going wage: "While few . . . can talk English, they somehow learn mighty quick what the price of labor is and they demand and get it; . . . they want as much as anybody else gets and won't work unless they are paid regulation wages."[9]

Thus the foreigner continued to come, and the law did not even prohibit his achieving the rank of miner; he often attained that position through conscientious hard labor. Inspector Williams completed his description of the actual work relation between the Slavic laborer and his Anglo-Saxon miner: "The Hun is anxious to learn, and the miner, in letting him drill for blasting and do other work that the ordinary laborer would not do, teaches him as much as he knows himself. The consequence is that after this kind of training the Pole or the Hun comes out a full-fledged miner and takes his place at the same rate of wages paid his other brethren."[10]

Finally the examinations for the mining certificate were hardly an obstacle to the non-English-speaking candidate. The exams were pretenses; interpreters were employed as coaches rather than translators. A traffic in certificates abounded, and some foremen even sold mining contracts to the highest bidder, whether or not the miner was certified.

So immigrants continued to flood the region. "This law was gotten up," said John Veith, the Reading's mining superintendent early in 1900, "to protect our people from the foreigners that came in, Hungarians and Polanders. . . . It did not work. . . . I have not seen an Irishman, or a German, or a Welshman, or an Englishman for the last ten years come in there, but the Hungarians and Italians have come in droves."[11]

117

Finally, some thought the law unnecessary as the Slavs' unsafe work habits had been exaggerated. A mine inspector dissented from the pronounced opinion of nativists and pointed out that the new immigrants killed one year were "working for more experienced English-speaking people." This situation "goes to show that there is as much, if not more thoughtlessness, . . . recklessness, indifference to danger, and contempt for [safety] among the intelligent and practical miners as there is among the less informed people of foreign lands."[12]

But continued support for an act keeps it a statute regardless of its effectiveness. Labor leaders and the prejudiced doggedly repelled any repeal. Such attempts failed in 1891, 1893, 1895, and 1897. Even a legislative report advocating a basic overhaul in the law had no better result.

Changes that were made strengthened the statute's principle. They stipulated that the experience had to be gained in Pennsylvania and stiffened the penalty to imprisonment. In 1901 a mining inspector still condemned the effect of this now-termed Gallagher law. He felt that it was keeping out the experienced worker and inviting the ignorant.[13]

Nevertheless the Anglo-Saxon mineworkers had their reasons for supporting the statute through the decade. A very important factor was the growing hostility toward the Slavs for their economic achievement. In the early 1890's especially the new immigrants' success in earning and saving money caused bitter resentment. The decade had been one of destitution, the worst depression the area ever experienced. Yet the Slavic community did not seem to suffer as did the Anglo-Saxon population.

Hard times and unemployment in the hard-coal districts had been particularly severe. Here the lack of work began earlier, around 1890, and was worse than in any other business in the state. In a normal year the anthracite mineworker labored somewhat over two hundred days on the average. But in the 1890's the mine-operating days read as follows for every second year: 200, 198, 190, 174, 152, and 166. The average in 1901 was 196.[14]

Distress then pervaded the hard coal region. In 1890, for example, the misery filled the Wyoming and southern districts especially. For the first three months the weekly employment was two days and the wage two dollars. Conditions forced storekeepers to allow much credit. Father O'Reilly of Shenandoah lamented that starvation rather than disease was causing the many doctors' calls among his parishioners. The town's seven major mines were then operating on three-quarter time.

In this chronic misery, however, the economic position of the Slavs differed from that of the rest. Even on their seventy-five cents a day they were still able to "save money, spend some in saloons, and buy property in a few years."[15]

Particularly in hard times such an achievement irritated the older groups. Rumors charged that the Huns and Poles even then bought their way into jobs. One Anglo-Saxon insisted that this East European economy was forcing others deeper into poverty: "There is scarcely a miner in Shenandoah, except he be a Hun or a Pole,

119

who is not in debt," for they "work for what our people cannot live on, and force [English-speaking] men who have families . . . to contract debts at the stores that some won't be able to pay for dear knows how long. . . . They are continually buying up property, yet they have money to spend in the saloons, too." A storekeeper acknowledged the comparative economic security of the Slav and concluded that at four to six dollars a week "the Huns . . . buy property, but how they do it is a mystery."[16] When visiting Wyoming, the same correspondent did not distinguish the nationalities in their degree of want, but here, too, the Slavs apparently fared better.

In 1894 the distress hit the northern region especially hard, with thirty thousand people, according to one reporter, verging on starvation. Yet again all did not face an empty larder, for "the Hungarians and Poles . . . are perhaps suffering the least during this period of depression."[17]

The state itself finally took action as the depression continued. The Governor appointed a committee to survey both the hard- and soft-coal regions and ascertain the extent of the misery. In the spring of 1897 the W. B. Meredith Committee visited several anthracite-district towns and interviewed 311 witnesses in twenty-seven sessions. Its findings did not equivocate: "Never . . . has the condition of the men employed in and about the mines been so deplorable or of such long duration."[18] But it still condemned the foreigners for sending large sums back to the old country. In addition, Balch testified to sizable real estate purchases by Polish and Slovak anthracite workers about that time.[19]

So the Slavs may have better weathered the buffeting economic winds through their willingness to work, but the Anglo-Saxons, mineworkers and nativists, could hardly have loved them for it. Politically more powerful than immigrant advocates, the older groups saw to it that the certificate-of-competency law stayed on the books.

The more realistic mineworkers recognized the hopelessness of bettering their lot through immigration restriction. Some believed that purely economic instruments, like unionization, had not really been given a chance to improve working conditions for the rank and file in the late 1880's. So when a trio of organizers from the United Mine Workers of America, a fledgling bituminous union, came into the anthracite region in 1894, labor hopes were reborn. And through the next years of trials and disappointments one of the three, John Fahy, would lead strike veterans to the sweetness of success.

But at first it seemed that management had little to fear from this union vanguard. The UMW was a small body, barely seventeen thousand members, and it still suffered from old internal divisions, for it stemmed from the combination of two older groups. The labor association had already designated the hard-coal region as District 1, but this was a hope more than a fact.

The necessity to begin organization in the anthracite districts became obvious during a soft-coal strike in mid-1894. In June, Local 538 of Gearhartsville, Clearfield County, noticed that anthracite coal was being substituted for bituminous coal. Sending John Rinn into the hard-coal region, the local petitioned UMW headquarters to give anthracite labor aid in their strike. Rinn saw

121

the unorganized condition of the region and asked the national body for a commission to start planting locals.

Even the most sympathetic union observers would have agreed that the little, boyish John Rinn, one hundred pounds, bald, and whiskerless, had an uncertain, Herculean task to perform. The picture of a four-year-old organization, recently divided internally, engaged in another strike, about to launch an organizational drive in hostile territory which was splintered ethnically would have dismayed the stoutest union heart. But Rinn made a good beginning by late July in placing locals in Mahanoy City and Shamokin. The miracle grew still more real as the organizer opened nine more branches before the second week in August. Encouraged, the national headquarters then sent two officers as aides, Vice-President Phil Penna and an executive board member, John Fahy. The achievement of the triumvirate must have surprised even themselves when Penna made a glowing report upon his return to union headquarters in Columbus. Two thousand mineworkers had signed up, and District 1 (anthracite) had been operating since August 24. The grateful members of the newly formed locals, now forty-four in number, elected Rinn as the district's first president in November. By the following month the UMW in the area consisted of nineteen more branches. The district prospered through 1895 and sent a good delegation to the national convention early in 1896.

The impossible had been accomplished. Once again the Schuylkill district led the others in welcoming regional organization. But the person who most rallied the

122

men to the union standard was John Fahy. For after replacing Rinn as district president in 1896, he remained in the anthracite region as the union leader, sometimes with help, sometimes alone, until the UMW established itself permanently in the industry in 1903.

Much of Fahy's success was due to personal characteristics, particularly a handsome appearance and pleasing manner. Slender, he looked taller than his five feet ten inches, and his generous mustache and large blue eyes emphasized his cleancut manliness. He was single, "one would imagine . . . from his own choosing," and as a woman commented later, clearly the "handsomest man in the union."[20] A "pleasing personality" matched his good looks, "calm, cool, and level-headed."[21]

These attributes plus a speaking ability and unflagging devotion helped him to accomplish the difficult task of organizing. At the peak of the enthusiasm during the district's second convention late in 1894, a *Journal* reporter mentioned Rinn's election but singled out Fahy's "untiring, energetic work and good counsel." The formal resolution of appreciation read, for his "untiring energy and unfaltering loyalty in the cause of downtrodden humanity in the anthracite coal field."[22] Secretary Doyle several weeks later stated that the large hard-coal representation at the coming national convention "is solely due to the untiring work of . . . John Fahy" and "[if he is not commended for] that merit which is due him, you will have sad hearts to mourn his turn-down in the anthracite field, where we have learned to admire and love him for his integrity, ability, honesty, and sincerity in working

123

for the cause."[23] Early the following year the men gave him their district's highest office.

Of course Fahy, Rinn, and the others did not have to begin their work in a completely anti-union environment. Certainly hard-coal figures, dedicated reformers, and other old-timers had kept alive the labor cause. Old Amalgamated veterans lent their assistance: John W. Parker of Mahanoy City, Dan Duffy, and even George Harris himself. Nevertheless the result was still a magnificent accomplishment for the UMW, particularly in winning the East European. The drawing of the Slavs to the colors even in the face of rank-and-file prejudice would have served as an omen to the operators in future strikes had they heeded it.

Fahy's youth and training in the ethnically diverse bituminous fields of Ohio undoubtedly prepared him well to weld the many nationalities into one organization. In fact the UMW itself had established procedures earlier for reaching the non-English-speaking peoples, like publishing the *Journal* in several foreign languages and using immigrant speakers at labor rallies. But despite the assistance of the union and local figures Fahy faced an ominous social situation, in essence an evident and growing separation of the Slavic and the Anglo-Saxon communities. His task was to inhibit widening divisions which were destroying the workers' unity.

Time only complicated the problem. The prosperity of the later 1890's increased the region's Slavic element and placed the sensitive ethnic balance in flux. Effective guidance and leadership of the work force came to demand ever more skill. But Fahy was equal to the effort; his strategy of carefully selecting foreign organizers, constantly using foreign languages in directives, encouraging sound nationality locals, and appointing Slavs to high positions established rank-and-file unity.

The immigrants received UMW organizers with surprising warmth. The larger Slavic communities required little labor propaganda. As early as 1894 the Shenandoah Lithuanians had begun a highly successful local that eventually numbered four thousand members. This group maintained itself so strongly that it established its own store. The Mt. Carmel Lithuanians acted largely on their own, too. They won the praise of an Anglo-Saxon who advised his more prejudiced friends that the Slavic local was "both a credit and an example to those who lay so much at the doors of the foreigners."[24] Mahanoy City and Hazleton also quickly formed foreign-language locals.

Fahy openly sought and encouraged new immigrant leaders. As district president, he planned "to throw his net for [more] Lithuanians and Polanders, having already . . . engaged speakers of these nationalities to accompany him, and assist in addressing and organizing."[25] His lieutenants were figures like District Vice-President Vitcufski, regional committee member Buliski, and the Polish vice-president of the Shamokin Subdistrict.

Thus with a spirited following and the nationality issue apparently no obstacle, the entire anthracite work force seemed about to enter the union ranks. But unhappily organization attempts suddenly halted. By the end of 1896 locals began to disband; Fahy's structure began

125

to crumble. The cause was neither a revived ethnic division nor an assault by employers, but the simple one of insufficient funds.

The shortage of cash for the unionizing drive had always hampered activities ever since the union entered the region in 1894. The workers' warm reception to their entrance may have pleased the three UMW heralds, Fahy, Rinn, and Penna, but the encouragement was more moral than financial. Laborers' income during this period was limited, and the more providential East Europeans hesitated to pay dues to a strange union. In addition UMW headquarters contributed little financial help after Penna's departure.

The anthracite district had actually run out of funds early in November, 1894. Fahy's three-dollar-a-day salary as executive board member and Rinn's fifty dollars per month as district president did not adequately compensate them for their organizing efforts.[26] Since August both had established locals on credit by sending the fee for credentials to the national organization from their own pockets.[27] At the second regional convention the district treasury had only $4.92. Fahy's Ohio friends wanted his salary increased when they heard in March, 1895, that the national owed him eight hundred dollars for his hard-coal endeavors. But the fact was that the union itself was not in good financial condition and had fewer than ten thousand paid members between 1894 and 1897.

So anthracite-area labor organization began to weaken in 1896.[28] At the district's February, 1897, meeting an unruly faction claimed that John Rinn's ten-dollar raise to sixty dollars per month was extravagant and forced the pioneer unionist out of office. Yet this action could not stay the irresistible drift toward insolvency. When the treasurer read the financial statement to Fahy later in the fall—collections $49.65, expenses $36.64, and on hand $13.01—the district president knew that the time had come for new strategy.[29]

No one can tell definitely why Fahy now forsook his organizing in the district. The work force had certainly not resisted unionization. The lack of funds may have been just too debilitating. At any rate, he sought a less expensive policy to aid mineworkers: lobbying in Harrisburg. It is entirely possible that the more nativist and prejudiced unionists convinced him that the best remedy for labor's problems was immigration restriction. Advocates may have repeated all the evils of the Slavic inundation.

Early in 1897 the Irish union leader traveled to the state capital to pressure the legislature for favorable restrictive bills. And he helped to pass an extension of miner certification, the Campbell Act. The new provisions discouraged immigrant employment by taxing any company hiring male aliens at the rate of three cents per day per head. The revenue would accrue to the county treasury, and the penalty imposed for noncompliance was stiff, up to a one-thousand-dollar fine for each offense. According to a report in the *United Mine Workers Journal* Fahy not only approved of the measure but felt the tax should have been higher.[30]

The Slavic Community on Strike

The young anthracite leader would surely have retracted his enthusiasm for the law had he known of one of its results: the killing of a score of Slavs and the wounding of twice that many. This disaster, called the Lattimer Massacre of 1897, is an event which even today stirs the passions of both the East European and the Anglo-Saxon populations. But the Lattimer riot's significance is not merely in the extent of the bloodletting but more in the circumstances surrounding the incident. For this was one of several outbreaks in the Lehigh field in which the Pole, Lithuanian, Slovak, and Ukrainian mineworkers *on their own* demonstrated in a series of strikes for economic justice.

This East European affair even forced John Fahy to forget his politicking and return to his original policy: that of planting the UMW standard throughout the anthracite region. From then on, with the momentum of Slavic enthusiasm, the UMW would unionize the entire industry.

VII

Lehigh in Turmoil

THE SOURCE OF THE IMMIGRANT PROTEST WAS A MINING
superintendent of the Lehigh and Wilkes-Barre Company
who took his job seriously. Gomer Jones had held supervisory positions in the industry for nineteen years; he
valued efficiency highly, and he had built a reputation for
cutting production costs, especially that of labor. When
he first noted the work pattern at the Honey Brook Colliery below Hazleton, the easygoing habits of the workers
irked him. He particularly could not tolerate the slowness
and inefficiency of the Slav.[1] "When I came here a year
ago [1896]," he said, "I came to restore discipline in the
mines and to operate them [profitably]. The discipline
was . . . lax. The men did about as they pleased. The
two superintendents here then associated with the men,
mixed with them, drank with them and were regarded as

129

'hail fellows well met.' . . . Now I cannot do that. I'm not a drinking man, and I've never made it a practice to hobnob with the men." His attitude was a strictly business one. "When I give orders I expect them to be obeyed. . . . I dismissed a good many men—about 80, I think—but I never put anybody in their places."[2] A policy change excited resentment, especially among the immigrants.

On about August 12, Jones posted a new work rule affecting mule drivers, chiefly Slavs and Italians. Since it meant additional work with no extra pay, a group of foreigners struck and demonstrated. When Jones went out to break up the picket line with a club, the strikers beat him until he managed to withdraw. *The Daily Standard* advised prophetically, "The outcome [of this dispute] will be watched with interest."

On the next workday the irate foreigners expanded the dispute and forced six company mines and three thousand employees to stop work. The leaders at a meeting of strikers that evening at McAdoo indicated the nationalities involved: a Slovak presided with an Italian assistant. The gathering resolved to submit their grievances to the head superintendent, Elmer H. Lawall. They particularly demanded Superintendent Jones' removal for his "tyrannical methods of ruling."[3] That same day a reporter circulated among the Slavic settlements with an interpreter to ascertain "the extent of the foreigners' reputed wrath." "Never in all our experience," he found, "have we met a more determined body of strikers than was found in the several patches."[4]

After a mixed Slavic–Anglo-Saxon committee met company officials and received no firm commitment, it returned to McAdoo to report. To a packed meeting at Mehalchick's Hall the representatives elaborated on the company's intentions *after* the men should return. The English-speaking element agreed to end the strike, but the immigrants reacted angrily and prohibited any resumption according to the *Wilkes-Barre Times* and the *Public Ledger*. However, Manager Lawall did end the stoppage by raising laborers' wages ten cents a day and revoking the original work rule.[5]

Resistance might have died here, but five hundred Slavs elsewhere struck the Van Wickle Company on August 27 over unfair pay discrimination. Here, too, it was the immigrants rather than the older nationalities who led the protest demonstrations. Their violent show of unity struck fear into the hearts of the Anglo-Saxon miners. "Three hundred foreigners, very few English-speaking men," marched from Coleraine and Beaver Meadow through Hazleton into Milnesville with clubs in hand. They intimidated Anglo-Saxons with their "yelling and shouting like base ball rooters when the score is tied in the thirteenth inning with two out and Kelly at bat."[6] The results of this protest were contagious. The immigrants renewed their fight with the L and WB, and others aliens struck a third operator, the Lehigh Coal and Navigation Company works. By September over five thousand pauper laborers had paralyzed the entire Hazleton area. The *Wilkes-Barre Times* dispatch on September 2 was hysterical: "Thousands of ignorant for-

131

eigners have begun a reign of terror, have closed up all the collieries, wrecked the home of the superintendent [Jones], and marched from one mine to another amid the wildest confusion, a howling mob without aim or leader."

The tumult and shouting were too much for Van Wickle, who offered his striking employees a raise. Unfortunately only some of his workers accepted it. By September 3 it was clear that the American and Anglo-Saxon mineworkers no longer could control the now-frequent immigrant demonstrations. Slavs and Italians seemed to enjoy the daily parades, as they tramped in a file behind an American flag, waved their clubs and iron bars, and scared off any nonstrikers whom they could find. One such incident occurred on the morning of the third and, because of its typical origin, resolution, and especially its vivid description, deserves close examination.

Just about dawn, on a field outside McAdoo, about three thousand strikers of the L and WB gathered to await Superintendent Lawall's response to their latest request to meet the Van Wickle raise. The sun rose and the passage of time increased the men's impatience. The eight-man committee, fearing violence, pleaded with their audience, largely Italians and Hungarians, to wait for the company's reply. But grumbling that followed was evidence of their impatience. Most of the crowd, now nine thousand strong, wanted action.

It was a spirited meeting, full of Italian and Hungarian curses, threats and insinuations. . . . At 10:30 the expected message had not arrived. . . . The committee reasoned, but of no avail, the miners were determined to give a demonstration. One burly Italian yelled at the top of his voice, "Whata da good of eighta da men do do'a the job? Too'a man'a! too'a man'a! I'a kill a Lawall better alone, d' [hell with] him." And to demonstrate that he meant what he said he drew forth a good sized carving knife and flourished it in the air yelling "Vendetta!"

This burst of Italian eloquence tended to invigorate the crowd and whisperings as to whether the committee were in sympathy with the men caused the able body of eight to evaporate. The Italian continued the matter in hand, "We getta do move on, and closa up the district," he said.

This suggestion was hailed with a yell and the brandishing of . . . pokers, bats, fence pickets, and small saplings. The American flag was brought out, unfurled and saluted by the enthusiastic [shouting] "America!"

The line of march was hastily laid out, squads were detailed to round up deserters and to impress on the milder sympathizers that in unity there was strength. To arms! With a mighty cheer and a waving of clubs the column moved. Down the main street of McAdoo an army of one thousand marched, cheered on by the shouts of loyal women and children. The most affecting sight was at a house on the outskirts of McAdoo, where a Hun too tired to march sought seclusion in the cellar of his house. But the keen [s]cent of the round-up squad ferreted him out and he was assisted into line on the end of eight clubs applied to his person in none too gently a manner. The scene was too affecting for his wife; she was assisted to her front yard and consoled by her sympathetic neighbors. There [were] many of these scenes along the line of march. The column moved on to Jeansville where a halt was called to give the "round up squads" time to join ranks. Then with a cheer the army de[s]cended on No. 1 breaker. [D]own through strippings, over culm banks, through groves and over fields came the army of strikers like an avalanche.

Hark! the deep-toned w[h]istle of the breaker announced the onslaught of the cavalcade and warned the working miners to defend themselves which they did by chasing out of the breaker and doing a hundred-yard dash over the adjacent hills. Hurrah! The breaker was won without a struggle, the enemy had fled. The Italians hooked a plank to the whistle leaving it blowing to announce the victory to the surrounding territory.

From the conquered breaker the army marched along the railroad track to Jeansville's main avenue. A halt was called and a discussion now arose as to whether it was best to march on to Hazleton.

Couriers were arriving with tales that the whole army of the United States and the militia of Pennsylvania were drawn up around Hazleton to protect the city from the approaching danger. This had little effect upon the body, but along the dusty highway, far away on the top of a distant hill was seen a speck. It was moving with the rapidity of lightning. Field glasses and all eyes were turned on it. There was a hush. 'Tis something important for no man would approach at such a killing pace if he had not news of the greatest importance. The Italian leader stood with bared head waiting.

The courier arrived. "Turn back! Turn back!" he shouted. "Why?" asked the leader. "You know not the danger awaiting you," exclaimed the breathless arrival. "Tell us!" shouted a thousand throats, "Tell us!"

"Hark ye then! Not over two miles from here on the outskirts of the city of Hazleton now stand the police force." There was an awful suspense. Aye, the police headed by the gallant captain, stand four . . . one wearing whiskers to defend the city.

The army trembled with fear. The whiskers [were] too much! The leader thought. He slowly raised his head and with a voice as steady as the earth on which he stood, exclaimed: "I gotta the right! I am a American citizen. I have my papers. They cannot stoppa us. Forward!" He pulled his naturalization papers from his pocket and wave[d them] aloft.

The army revived. Enough! They were protected and with one throat the vast army yelled, "On to Hazleton!"

With a calm and determined step the miners marched on to Hazleton. It was a grand and [glorious] sight; fully three thousand five hundred strong. This noble array of lower European chivalry approached the beautiful city of Hazleton. There is a gradual des[c]ent from the mountain which enabled the citizens of the city of pits to observe the strength of the approaching foe.

Hazleton was in a fevered heat of excitement, the bolder of the inhabitants had gathered on the environs behind the resolute body of the police, four strong, whose stars glistened in the bright sun.

The captain of the police approached the strikers. They halted and he was heard to explain in resolute tones. "Why come ye here? Disperse ye agitators of the peace." The leader of the strikers with a voice equally as resolute as the captain's explained: "Getta outa de way. We noa stoppa!"

135

The undismayed captain replied: "Disperse or I'll run ye in!"

"Ha, ha," laughed the leader of the strikers as he pulled papers from his pocket. "I am a Americano citizen. I a defia you. We a goa through your a city."

The captain seeing with what terrible power the leader of the strikers was armed suggested arbitration.

"Nita! Nita!" explained the leader. "We a go through the outskirts of the city toa Hazle Mine." The brave captain saw a chance to avoid conflict and suggested that he and his noble array of police accompany the strikers through the city so that they could not become lost in the various hiways and byways. The offer was accepted and the column again moved.

After the array had passed through the city it halted for the charge on the Hazle breaker. The ready telephone had got in its work, however, for as they broke from the city the deep-toned whistle announced the approach of danger and the breaker miners vacated within six seconds.

Victory! The strikers had again won the day. This was not all their laurels for soon after Cranberry and Hazle Brook followed the fate of No. 1 and Hazle breakers.

'Twas a grand stroke to march eleven miles and close up four breakers. Napoleon's greatest achievements were overshadowed. And as the setting sun cast its last ray over the distant mountain the grand army of striking Huns, Italians and Slavs marched to their homes to enjoy the calm and quiet peace after a day of war.[7]

Noteworthy here was not merely the fact of exclusively immigrant involvement. The demonstration also indi-

136

cates the reason for such a belligerent protest. When once the mob agreed to "closa up the district," the discipline had an awe-inspiring militancy. As the account noted, a few less enthusiastic "Huns" tried to sneak home, but the "round-up squads assisted" them back "into line on the end of eight clubs in none too gently a manner." The suggestion is that the immigrant communal structure, the patch, would not tolerate division or dissension of any sort, especially in its external relations with its employer. Years before the peasant Slavs had recognized the strength of group, rather than individual, action in building their parish in America. When an arbitrary foreman or intolerable conditions affected them, they reacted as a community, en masse. To Americans the strike was mainly an economic protest; to the Slavs it indeed was more like "war."

Meanwhile public anxiety mounted as immigrant dissatisfaction spread and local authorities could not maintain order. Townspeople felt somewhat relieved when on September 5 all the victorious Van Wickle men returned. But a workers' representative warned Lawall of heavy immigrant pressure: "If you cannot give the A. S. Van Wickle advance, committee will no longer exist. Answer at once." The L and WB superintendent leisurely forwarded the message to superiors.[8] Immigrant unrest continued at Silver Brook, Hazle Mines, and elsewhere.

The sheriffs of surrounding counties—James Martin of Luzerne, Setzer of Carbon, and Scott of Schuylkill—finally gathered a thousand men in armed posses to break up the immigrant marches, and the Winchesters that they carried did dampen strike enthusiasm. Yet continuing

137

incidents kept county officials busy directing their "army" to meet the belligerent "Hungarians." One report noted a typical confrontation where "the foreign element [including women and children] composed the principal portion of the marching army." After some difficulty, Sheriff Martin and fifty deputies forced them to disperse before Cranberry breaker number 6.[9]

It was as a result of such a demonstration that the infamous Lattimer Massacre took place. A group of Poles, Lithuanians, and Slovaks marched from Harwood to close down the Pardee Company's Lattimer Mine. When they arrived, they met Sheriff Martin and an armed posse, who ordered them to disperse. The next few moments are unclear, but Martin either fell or was pushed and ordered his deputies to shoot either at the strikers or above their heads. The posse fired directly into the unarmed marchers, who, screaming, ran for cover.

As soon as townspeople heard the shooting, many rushed to the fallen strewn about the field. Eleven already dead were sent to the morgue, and the wounded were conveyed to the hospital. Martin and his deputies evaporated unnoticed.

The exact number shot is unknown, but the casualty list eventually reached about nineteen dead and thirty-nine wounded. Their backgrounds were an East European mixture: twenty-six Poles, twenty Slovaks, and five Lithuanians.[10]

At the Hazleton hospital and morgue the tragedy continued. Frantic, kerchiefed women, trailing bewildered children behind, searched among the blood-spattered beds for their husbands and sons. When they found the ones they sought, a pitiable wailing arose. A tired Reverend Richard Aust, pastor of the nearby Polish St. Stanislaus Church, arrived from the Lattimer field where he had been administering the last rites. He continued attending the dying and wounded at the hospital and tried to console the women lamenting in the morgue.

Fears of the Slavic community's reaction created hysteria among English-speaking groups. The entire Lattimer settlement with one exception fled their homes; they took their bedding to the homes of friends or slept out in the open on the other side of the hill.

State authorities now were called in. On a plea from Sheriff Martin for troops, Governor Hastings sent General J. P. S. Gobin and the Third Brigade. When the commander arrived with most of his twenty-five hundred men early the next morning, "the English-speaking people [were] overjoyed, for now they can retire for the night with the assurance that all will be well."[11]

The entire Lattimer affair suggests, as preceding incidents did, that the outbursts were immigrant manifestations of community sentiment. Harwood, a Slavic patch, had decided on the march in the first place, despite sheriffs' threats, warnings, and pleas for peace. The Slavs regarded their cause as a crusade for justice that permitted little compromise.

The group nature of the "Hungarian" protests was evident, too, in the reaction to the massacre. First, despite General Gobin's admonition to eschew ceremony, East Europeans demonstrated their grief in magnificent funer-

139

als.[12] All that day and the next, sightseers poured into Hazleton on foot, bicycle, wagon, and trolley to see the battlefield and the coming ceremony. The visitors were to view a rare sight, for the immigrants emphasized their deep indignation and bereavement at the funerals on Sunday and Monday. Father Aust and Slavic Lutheran Reverend Carl Hauser waited at St. Joseph's Slovak Church in Hazleton for three bodies to be brought from Harwood and Humboldt.

The day's weather supplied the perfect background for what took place. Through a fine, chilling drizzle and a heavy mist, a brass band playing the death march led the cortege. With muffled drums it preceded the three biers, the families of the deceased, and a thousand paraders in grocery and beer wagons past culm piles crowded with fascinated onlookers. Prominent in the snake-like procession wending its way along the road was a double file of men and boys of St. Joseph's Society wearing red, white, and blue sashes on their shoulders and crepe badges over their hearts. The brightly colored uniforms of the participating Societa Italia-Americano contrasted with the drab "In Memoriam" patches on their arms. Mineworkers and their families, dressed in their best, completed the train and, reaching the church, filled it to capacity.

Spectators watched a similar sight on Monday, the thirteenth, the service for the Polish and Lithuanian dead. Three more bodies rode in another cortege from Harwood, this time behind St. Kazimir's Cornet Band of Audenried and before fifteen hundred marchers.

Father Martyczus received them at St. Peter's and Paul's Lithuanian Church in West Hazleton. Meanwhile Father Aust had a platform erected in front of St. Stanislaus' altar to accommodate the nine coffins of Poles carried from the undertakers. After the Requiem Mass the twelve were buried in St. Stanislaus' cemetery before a throng of six thousand.

The ostentatious laying away of the Lattimer victims did not allay the Slavs' bitterness toward Sheriff Martin and his deputies. The marchers had been unarmed and the posse had shot most of the strikers in the back. Above all, the resulting misery of fatherless families, the widows and orphans, cried out for retribution and compensation. The massacre's impact on Slavic America was an unprecedented unanimity in defense of the victims and an attack on the authorities. The Ukrainian *Svoboda* of Mt. Carmel labeled the fray clear "murder," an example of the "bestiality" of American deputies. The organ of the recently formed Polish National Catholic Church, *Straż,* saw the affair as America's refusal to grant justice to honest workmen. Its report concluded with an appeal for a workingman's party.

East Europeans also condemned Martin at large, open-air rallies. At Shenandoah, Shamokin, Scranton, and Mt. Carmel thousands gathered to offer material aid for the prosecution. At Nanticoke, Polish priests forbade demonstrations, so the Slavs, led by wealthy Emil Malinowski, placed a declaration of aid in local newspapers.

The occurrence assumed even national significance. Sympathetic conventions took place outside the hard-coal area throughout Slavic settlements along the Great Lakes and in the Northeast. The Polish National Alliance, the Lithuanian Alliance, the Polish-Lithuanian League of New York, a Russian labor society in Philadelphia, and Baltimore, Chicago, and Connecticut Lithuanians expressed their outrage and pledged thousands of dollars in financial assistance.

The Austro-Hungarian Government made the affair an international incident. The Ambassador sent a consul secretary into the fields from Philadelphia to collect affidavits. Repeatedly for over a year the emissary through diplomatic channels insisted upon compensation, but to no avail.

With the victims laid to rest, the anthracite-region Slavs established a permanent body to handle the donations for relief and court costs, the "National Prosecuting and Welfare Committee of the Lattimer Victims." Father Aust was in charge, and John Nemeth, a Polish merchant of Hazleton, acted as treasurer. The outcome of the five-week trial of Martin and his men was a finding of not guilty.[13] Yet even the Slavs' disappointment was a unified expression.

Meanwhile the many strikes in the area continued and reached their height by September 14. Almost eleven thousand men and fifteen mines of Coxe Brothers, Lehigh Valley, L and WB, Van Wickle, and Pardee were not working. One company's directive to its mule drivers had indeed created a storm.

The next developments were the denouement. With just one exception the companies offered some improvement to the strikers, either higher pay or better conditions.

The men, largely Anglo-Saxon, were returning to work in numbers by the sixteenth.

Yet even at this point immigrant resistance continued, this time in the form of Slavic womanhood, or rather a stronger-willed leader, "Big Mary" Septek. In the waning days of the strike Mrs. Septek's behavior was another expression of immigrant feeling and recalled the Shenandoah riots of 1888. This husky female led the Slavic community, which still sought complete victory, in attacking any workers returning to the mines.

Mary had already gained an influential position as a community leader. Known for her forceful character, she ran, or perhaps ruled, a boardinghouse of sixteen men near the Lattimer company store. When word of the resumption reached her patch, "Big Mary" recruited a brigade of Slavic women to chase returnees home. Violence again was rife. At five separate points on September 16 a score of women armed with clubs, rolling pins, and pokers led over a hundred men and boys in chasing immigrant workers on the south side. The next day "a wild band of women swooped down" on two hundred washery workers, who fled.[14]

The incidents bewildered the authorities. General Gobin, charged with maintaining order, was "in a quandary over the foreign women raids" and the problem of how to deal with the "Amazons."[15] And *The Wilkes-Barre Record* criticized the unseemly behavior of immigrant femininity:

> The appearance of women as a factor in a coal region strike is a novelty of a not very pleasing nature. Those who have made themselves so con-

143

spicuous the past week in . . . the Hazleton region were the wives, mothers, and sisters of the Hungarian, Polish and Italian strikers, and it is assumed that they had the sanction of their husbands, sons and brothers in their ill-advised and unwomanly demonstrations.[16]

The reporter mourned the passing of better times when "such scenes would have been impossible in the troubles between capital and labor . . . when our mines were manned by English-speaking men. . . . This . . . is only another . . . forcible illustration of the great change that has taken place in these coal regions since the importation of cheap European labor commenced."

The strength of Polish womanhood could not withstand military force and the growing back-to-work sentiment. Gobin's troops broke up one of Big Mary's sallies near Lattimer while a heavy guard escorted twenty-five hundred L and WB mineworkers to their jobs. Elsewhere, even immigrants began to yield; all mines were operating by October 4. Natives undoubtedly welcomed the peace, and even the immigrant community received some additional satisfaction: although some confusion resulted, the courts declared one of the chief provocations, the Campbell Act, unconstitutional.

The other two fields had not followed the Lehigh suspension with their own. The Wyoming men were still poorly organized, although generally well paid. The Schuylkill Slavs did consider going out in sympathy, but the Reading's better treatment of its employees and the company's mid-September suspension of Campbell Law deductions were probably the major deterrents.

One person especially had welcomed the labor disturbances. True, he regretted the violent excesses, but when the outbreaks began, the President of District 1 of the UMW took approving note of an aroused rank and file. The Slavic-inspired unrest gave John Fahy and his almost-moribund organization a renewed opportunity for recruitment. At the first sign of trouble the Irish labor leader left Harrisburg and rushed back to the pits. The result was all he hoped for, a strong and secure foothold in Lehigh.

Throughout, Fahy's policy in the region won the compliments of all, both Anglo-Saxon and Slav. While propagandizing for his cause, he constantly urged the strikers to avoid violence. And for his moderate counsel the older nationalities respected him. On the other hand, he also won Slavic favor when he established more foreign locals and selected good immigrant leaders.

It was the spirited Lehigh and Wilkes-Barre employees who first brought Fahy back to the region. In mid-August a number of them sent the Irish organizer a message asking that he begin establishing UMW branches. At his arrival on August 19 the mineworkers overwhelmed him by their reception—the hired hall was too small for his audience, so the meeting was moved to a nearby baseball field, where over a thousand mineworkers sat down to listen to his address. After exhorting the strikers but cautioning against violence, he immediately organized the first UMW local in Lehigh. A week later the labor leader enlisted over two thousand members

145

in many additional branches. In addition Fahy assisted the employees' committee in negotiations with Lawall.

The union leader had to return to the state capital on business, but the mineworkers refused him a long absence. Van Wickle's Coleraine strikers and those at Beaver Meadow and Silver Mine telegraphed Fahy several times to return and give them locals, too. With the Irishman's reappearance, many collieries sought his services. Journalists affirmed that he had never been so busy.

The burgeoning crisis below Hazleton dismayed the district chief, and he advised caution in his speeches, especially to his immigrant listeners. He dwelt on the presence of the sheriffs and their posses, and the possible consequences of disorder. Nevertheless, some ignored his warnings, and once Fahy even had to disperse a march himself. "The [Audenried] strikers or the foreign leaders at least showed that they had not relinquished their determination to march this morning." Just when they started out from Blaine Street, the

> general organizer . . . John Fahy . . . exhorted the men to give attention to his pleas for peace. He was howled down. Again he tried to be heard but with the same result. . . . The line moved on down through the borough. Mr. Fahy was determined. . . . He hastened to the end of the line again and waving a copy of the evening newspaper containing the sheriff's proclamation commanded them to listen. This time he was successful in checking the onward march. Mr. Fahy pleaded with them [and] read the . . . riot act which was but imperfectly understood. . . . [It] was impressed upon them and

they seemed for the first time to realize that the majesty of the law was supreme. . . . Then the men decided to break ranks . . . [and go] to their homes.

Mr. Fahy performed an excellent service on this occasion.[17]

Undoubtedly the labor leader dreaded a repetition of the Lattimer killings as much as any responsible figure. He saw, too, that the union's interest was involved, for the employers could now more easily link the UMW to agitation, violence, and bloodshed. At a Slavic gathering on Donegal Hill after the September 7 incident, the Irishman followed the Slovak, Polish, and Ruthenian curates in again begging his audience to maintain order. Yet, however much he abhorred bloodshed, he had to admit that the shooting did publicize organization. The *Evening Herald* noted in mid-September that "organizer John Fahy" was still "in great demand," particularly at a Lattimer rally where immigrants enlisted en masse.

By the end of the strike Fahy's position could not have been more advantageous. He had expanded the union with public commendation: "John Fahy, president of the Anthracite United Mine Workers of America is receiving high praise on every hand for the way he has worked since the beginning of the troubles"; "President Fahy . . . is today better thought of and more respected by the entire community than any other leader of the laboring men who has entered the anthracite coal fields"; "His course . . . is highly commended on all sides. He did signal service in keeping the men from acts of violence."[18]

The *United Mine Workers' Journal* probably claimed

147

too much when in November it announced that Fahy had planted locals "in every patch and every hamlet" in the Lehigh district. But the true extent of Fahy's good work appeared at the next UMW national convention in January at Columbus. The Pennsylvania anthracite district then had sixty-four locals in all, the second district in size to Illinois (which had seventy-two). And Lehigh boasted almost half the total. It became a completely separate district, Number 7, in mid-1898. Fahy could now devote his energies to the last region to be won, the north.

Along with Fahy other contributors must be recognized. It must be noted that the Slavs initiated the 1897 protest; in fact the entire upheaval from mid-August through September was immigrant led. Throughout, from Honey Brook to Lattimer and beyond, it was the East European grievance that kept the strike alive.

The spontaneity of their behavior was particularly surprising. Oddly, no continuous immigrant leadership emerged or was evident. Most workers seemed to have walked off their jobs according to a grass roots consensus. The *Wilkes-Barre Times* on September 16 summarized the conflict:

> The petty disagreement between the Lehigh and Wilkes-Barre Company mule drivers and their employers now affects . . . a majority of the principle [sic] [operators] in the middle coal fields. It is one of the most peculiar strikes ever inaugurated. The miners have no organization and in many instances don't know exactly what they struck for except to say that they feel they have been unfairly treated.

Brandishing their fence paling, their new citizenship papers, and the American flag in long lines headed for working mines, the Slavs did understand and respond to injustice.

One can only speculate again, as similarly to 1888, on the Slavs' greater willingness to strike, the contagion of their unrest, and their militancy in battle. Their settlements were tightly knit communal entities in close communication with each other. When one patch decided to strike, its inhabitants quickly broadcast their feelings to countrymen elsewhere to have them join in the protest. If the other patches had grievances, they would accept the invitation and pass on the strike demand to others. It was such a Slavic chain reaction that caused Lattimer and broadened the dispute.

Also, as in the 1888 affair, within each parish a purge of dissenting immigrant mineworkers went on, as is evidenced by the dynamited homes, the assaults on individuals, and the other attacks. Thus when the Slavic locality went on the march, it did so with a terrible ferocity and unity. Such active expression included not just the breadwinners but all members of the community, particularly women and children.

Here in Lehigh the results of the foreign strikers' recklessness, too, were noteworthy. First, the martyrdom of the Lattimer victims bound Slavic local and some national organizations even closer together vis-à-vis the external American environment. Responsible, nonmineworking East European leaders now more readily defended workers' rights and branded Martin and his men as murderers.

Second, and of more interest, the foreign strikers, although almost leaderless, did on the whole win their point. The immigrant enthusiasts who predominated at the height of the struggle were able to force many of the operators to grant concessions.

In addition, the violent outbreaks stimulated the more hesitant English-speaking rank and file to action. At first the Anglo-Saxons did not support the immigrants. The determination of the Slavs, however, not only disciplined their own dissenters but may very well have intimidated the other nationalities. Event after event proved that the older groups did not want to strike; in instances where they did go out, the Slavic resistance kept them idle longer than they wished. One newspaper's view of the nationality involvement was typical just after Lattimer: "The Hungarian-Pol[ish]-Italian element are very strong in their determination not to work. If the matter were left to the English-speaking miners, the collieries would likely be able to start any time."[19] The fact is that the Irish, Welsh, and English did not begin interesting themselves in the strike until after mid-September.

Finally, and most important, the East European unrest brought back the UMW to anthracite. Of course, "Hungarian" dissatisfaction was an invitation to the union. Fahy arrived on the scene early and to the best of his ability, which was outstanding, utilized the discontent to construct a new and sound base for his organization. But again, the strike was mainly the Slavs', not the UMW's.

Perhaps the most aptly expressed moral of the entire struggle came from a nearby newspaper. With the Lehigh field still a shambles, a score dead, perhaps a hundred injured, and thousands of dollars of property damaged, the Elmira, New York, *Telegraph* offered a moral to the superintendent whose new work rule caused the initial protest: "Gomer has learned a lesson. He has been taught a man is a man even if he is a Hungarian."[20]

as an intermediary between the region's newer and older nationalities. Undoubtedly he understood the area well from having worked in the mines twenty years from the age of nine. He also was a respected figure within Polonia, particularly the result of a "likeable personality." And finally he considered himself very much an American. While the son of Polish parents, he had been born in 1869 in the United States, so that he was one of the first native Polish-Americans.

Fahy also contacted other likely immigrant organizers. He recognized that John Bednarski of Shenandoah "has much influence with foreign speaking peoples . . . especially Polanders" and had him brought into union meetings. Other Slavic assistants included a Polish-speaking Frenchman, Cornell S. Pottier, also of Shenandoah, and John Feleski.

Thus in 1900 District 9 was as strongly situated as was Wyoming District 1. Fahy and Pulaski by June had built the district to fifty-five affiliates. In a progress report Secretary George Hartlein stated that Fahy's enthusiasm was "certainly hustling things," and he concluded by commending President Mitchell "for sending organizers of such good quality as Bro. Pulaski."[11]

Now that the organization had grown beyond its early stages, the more aggressive locals began to insist on a stronger stand with the operators. The northern workers particularly sought working conditions equivalent to the more liberal arrangement in Schuylkill. When the regional companies ignored their demands in the early months of 1900, the Wyoming representatives urged

159

President Mitchell to declare a general anthracite-district suspension.

So the pressure on the UMW administration for action mounted. President Mitchell, however, regarded strikes seriously and their use as the last extremity, and the other district presidents did not yet wish to risk their recent expansion in conflict. So Mitchell advised the northern representatives that any industrywide demonstration would have to wait until later in the summer.

By August the northerners forced a tri-district meeting to draw up a list of grievances to be presented to the operators. When the mineowners refused to negotiate, Mitchell reluctantly issued a general strike call to take effect September 17.

With a paid-up regional membership of only eight thousand, the union's hesitation is not hard to understand. But the work of Fahy, Evans, James, and the Slavic organizers since the 1897 strike had not been ineffectual, and an increasing involvement of the immigrant community during the two years can be discerned. In this first industrywide strike their behavior showed a determined loyalty to the union, or more exactly to the union cause.

The immediate response to the call by at least eighty thousand mineworkers surprised even the most hopeful unionists.[12] But it should not have been entirely unexpected; the eight thousand UMW members were only a part of the many who would follow union directions. At any rate the total number idle filled the union headquarters with joy, and with his characteristic enthusiasm

Fahy congratulated Mitchell: "Congratulations, old man, she's a beaut and all it needs is to continue for a short time as it has been and then sure as the stars shine above tonight I feel we're a winner and O Lord! won't we shout and jubilate."[13]

The response of each district obviously reflected past dissatisfaction. Wyoming, which had pushed for the contest and largely formulated the demands, went out nearly unanimously, but the two lower regions received the summons coolly. Hardly half of the work force there obeyed the order. Either they had no real grievance or they had not been organized. Essentially, then, the demands of the workers were Wyoming ones.

Yet in a very short time the organizers' past educational work and the discipline of the East Europeans began to pull everyone into the fray. Despite the supposed handicaps of nationality and regional divisiveness, the UMW had laid its groundwork well. For the first time in history, anthracite labor in all three districts was unified, and in a short time the response was complete. Two days after the call three-quarters of the Lehigh workers were out, and five thousand more in Schuylkill had struck. By the end of the week the total idle reached 125,000, and on October 4 the maximum, 97 percent of the work force.

Had the operators had their way, they would have drawn out the battle into economic war with the union. But the Republican party's national chairman, Mark Hanna, felt that such a strike would hurt McKinley's chances in the coming election, and he forced the mine-

161

owners to make concessions. So rather suddenly on October 1 two leading companies declared an immediate 10 percent wage increase and negotiation on other items. After some additional bargaining, and employers' concessions, the union called the men back to work at the end of October.

Thus the operators gave in. A temporary victory went to the union (the agreed-upon terms were to last only to April, 1901). True, the UMW had not yet achieved outright recognition, but some experts marveled at the union's discipline over the entire work force. The labor organization had shut down the mines almost completely after the first few days.[14]

Enlarged membership rolls were another result of the union's success. By January, 1901, the three anthracite districts had grown 600 percent, fifty-three thousand over the previous year, probably much of the increase after August.[15] Certainly the prestige of the labor organization had risen greatly among the rank and file.

Finding reasons for the labor success is deceptively easy. The shortness of the strike and outside pressure on the operators to yield really hid two other factors. One was completely new, the leadership of the union president, Johnny Mitchell, and the other was the already well-known conduct of the East European community.

Even before the strike began, Mitchell as president had won much outside praise for his conservative philosophy. He earnestly believed in social justice for all classes, yet such reform to him was to be nonrevolutionary and particularly nonviolent. Strangely enough for a labor leader, he disliked work stoppages: "I am opposed to strikes as I am opposed to war," he said; "the world is in no mood to tolerate leaders of labor organizations who foment strife . . . over trivial grievances or through the mere professional love of trouble."[16]

In following those principles in the 1900 strike he added to his public stature. He had striven for and won favorable public opinion, for it was important to him that unions be generally accepted. He secured such approbation by warning the men against violence, approving heartily of the temperance pledge, and refusing to call out the maintenance men—a step that would have meant much property destruction. Always close to the clergy, the UMW leader also made a special effort to woo the church, particularly Bishop Hoban of Scranton. His personal achievement was, then, important. "Retention of favorable public sentiment was no easy task. It was chiefly due to the avoidance of violence, the conciliatory attitude of John Mitchell, . . . his skillful presentation of the issues, and his appeal to justice and fair play."[17]

Surprisingly enough, with all his moderation before the public, Mitchell was extraordinarily popular among his own, the anthracite-region workers, both immigrant and native. The explanation for this rank-and-file attachment is really enigmatic and indefinable, but it was probably connected with Mitchell's own attractive character. Outwardly modest, his very appearance exuded confidence, dignity, and integrity. He was a handsome, clean-shaven figure whose neatly combed hair and youth (thirty-one in 1900) earned for him the titles "Boy President" and "Old Young Man." His usual dress, a clerical-like garb with long black coat, black tie, and high white collar, made him look sober and reserved. Whatever feature of his character magnetized his men, the workers welcomed him as a triumphant hero after the strike. "On the occasion of President Mitchell's visit to Scranton, Wilkes-Barre, Shamokin, Shenandoah and Mt. Carmel the demonstrations held eclipsed anything ever before held in those cities." And Paul Pulaski accompanied five hundred men who walked the fifteen miles from Shamokin to Pottsville to take part in a reception of twenty-five thousand in honor of their chief.[18] Even Mitchell's most hated opponent, operator John Markle, admitted: "This success of Mitchellism invited every class of labor in the anthracite region . . . to form unions. . . . Mitchell was placed on a pinnacle. The Laborers . . . believed he could accomplish anything."[19] And finally the gratitude of admirers took material form, a medallion from the breaker boys, a 325-dollar loving cup from the Scranton Elks, a silver-mounted umbrella from the Archbald schoolteachers, a gold-headed cane from union officials, and a gold clock and two candelabra from immigrant locals.

While the image of their president gave the men something to honor during and after the struggle, another factor in the strike had a more immediate impact, the activity of the Slavic colony. In such a largely unorganized industry, a strong, militant force of strikers was necessary to bring out the workers and keep them idle.

164

The East European family and community sentiment once again enforced discipline.

The first task for the immigrants was assuring that all obeyed the strike call. Wyoming's response was almost unanimous, as noted, and more important, the Slavic community in the two more apathetic areas, too, was loyal to the strike. In the more strongly organized Hazleton area "the foreign speaking miners are in the majority . . . and most of them are in favor of a strike. The English speaking workmen who are in favor of striking are not as numerous."[20]

Lower Lehigh, however, worked on. This area far below Hazleton in Panther Creek Valley had always been isolated and never organized. It, too, had a loyal immigrant minority, but according to the *Public Ledger* the entire foreign element in the valley would not have been strong enough to close the collieries even had they all gone out.

In Schuylkill, the southern district, ethnic backgrounds again divided the eager from the hesitant. The heavily Polish Shamokin-Mt. Carmel area was "tied tighter than ever before in its history."[21] In contrast stood the one non-Slavic hamlet of Ashland, "where there are none of the undesirable class of foreigners that are making trouble in the other districts, the men here are all American, Irish, Germans, and Welsh, none of them members of the Mine Workers' organization."[22]

Unfortunately tensions and threats arose in the other large immigrant concentrations. At Mahanoy City the Lithuanians could not agree to strike with the East

Europeans, and the English-speaking miners were indifferent. District official Paul Pulaski rushed there and exhorted his people at a mass meeting of more than a thousand on Sixth Street. There the "Poles, Slavs, Hungarians, and Lithuanians unanimously resolved to strike," although the next day only three thousand did so; many of the Lithuanians were still holding back.[23] Time would tell if the pressure of immigrant strikers would win this community.

Shenandoah, the model melting pot, had changed for the worse since the last Schuylkill strike. The population had grown 50 percent to about twenty thousand, now two-thirds Slavic, with the immigrants jammed into the "Rocks" section. Pottier and Pulaski had gone among the shanties with good results—UMW strength was composed chiefly of Poles and Lithuanians. With the contest brewing, the town paper summarized the sentiment of Slav and Anglo-Saxon: "Almost all the English speaking people, as distinguished from the Poles, Lithuanians and Austrians [perhaps Slovaks], expressed themselves as opposed to a strike."[24]

The sense of the foreign community was really not clear to the *Herald,* especially when the immigrant priest, Father Lenarkiewicz, condemned any work stoppage. Probably under his influence the Poles in preliminary local meetings voted against a strike. But apparently the East Europeans were deeply split, for on Wednesday, September 19, they reversed the decision and resolved to stop work. On Thursday, when only a part of the workers were idle, the Slavs' mighty community power went into operation. Their action took the form of "flying squads" to intercept would-be workers.

Just at dawn on the morning of the twenty-first townspeople noted groups of immigrants congregating along the streets. One group halted a trolley bound for the mines, pulled off the twenty passengers inside, who were for the most part English, Irish, and Americans, and beat and stoned them as they fled. Another group of strikers smashed the windows and doors of Kehley Run Colliery and drove out the two hundred workers. Other squads of belligerent immigrants forced Kohinoor, West Shenandoah, Shenandoah City, and Turkey Run collieries to cease working.

At this point the ever-present coal-and-iron police, the mine guards, began to offer resistance and protect workers. The result now took a human toll, particularly at Indian Ridge, where Slavs and police exchanged gunfire. When county authorities arrived on a call from mining officials, a deputy sheriff described their reception: "The Poles came out of their quarters as thick as flies. We were cornered [near the railroad] station and we backed up and fought!" When the officers finally did get through the mob, "they were throwing things at us from all the houses—crockery, beer bottles, anything."[25]

Meanwhile another body of deputies engaged in an uglier exchange at the Indian Ridge mine. Several thousand men, a majority of whom were Lithuanians according to the *Plain Speaker,* pelted them with eggs and stones. When Sheriff Toole attempted to escort some workers home, a gun battle ensued, which ended only after a Pole had been killed and seven others wounded. The names of seven casualties indicate the nationalities involved: Koniski, Wendick, Scarin, Sanlis, Yuliski, Blozik, and Feriski. Elsewhere strikers injured were Stalmochowicz, Wudinchry (possibly Wudicki), Savitsky, Axalavage, Sevoloski, Beniunis, and Skamawicz. Those assaulted by rioters were Evans, Knoth, Fry, Edwards, Rowlands, Bitting, and others, all of whom clearly had non-Slavic names.

The day's events horrified Shenandoah. Besides the usual property damage the final toll was two dead and a score injured. And since authorities had not restored order, few dared venture into the streets. News spread that the "Rocks" people were determined to stop all work the next day, too. "Excitement runs high, there may be another clash at any time. The foreigners are greatly incensed and threaten to cause further trouble. . . . Many swore they would wipe out all the English speaking people in the town."[26]

That evening a frightened borough council closed all the saloons, swore in an additional two hundred fifty deputy police, and appealed to Governor Stone for troops. Once again the Chief Executive sent in a familiar visitor, General Gobin, with twenty-one hundred men.

With the presence of National Guardsmen, the townspeople felt bold enough to criticize the Slavic element, particularly the Lithuanians, for the disorder. The East Europeans had overruled moderate sentiment "by the aid of a bludgeon," defied law, and "seemed to utterly disregard the value of human life." The well-known Irish priest, Father O'Reilly, warned in a sermon that the perpetrators would "encounter a day of reckoning."

On the other hand, the real heroes to the townspeople were the English-speaking mineworkers. They had even volunteered for the posse and were considered to be among the most reliable deputies. Sheriff Toole himself testified to the role of the two nationality groups: "[The trouble] was caused by foreigners alone. The English speaking miners behaved splendidly and many of them were at my back risking their lives to maintain order."[27]

Even unionists added their criticism of the "Hungarians." One deputy who was also a striker emphasized that the posse, mostly miners like himself, would protect the town with their lives. "Our wives and babies are here and we will kill those foreigners if they resort to [further] violence." He sympathized with the immigrants' goal, a successful strike, "but rioting will not win it."[28]

The union organization voiced the same opinion. The local UMW leaders insisted that they did not favor such outbreaks and were doing everything possible to prevent them. But the unionists must have noted the effectiveness of the Slavic-inspired riots. The intimidation of nonstrikers had spread far and wide. Even before the eventful day ended, the Reading announced that as a result of the riot five more collieries would not work the next day.

Meanwhile, on Monday, a feeling of outrage was evident among the entire Slavic community at the funeral for a dead striker. This laying-to-rest of one deceased normally affected the community deeply; the peasant mind grieved not only for the loss but also over burial in alien soil, far from his village. Moreover, here in Shenandoah was the added sentiment that their countryman died for a cause, justice at the work place. Just as at the Lattimer ceremony three years before the East Europeans gave their hero another martyr's burial. St. George's Lithuanian brass band led thousands, including members of Polish and Lithuanian societies wearing black crepe, in a slowly moving file along the main road. The line of march stopped at the deceased's hovel, where the men all raised their hats while the hearse moved to the front. The mourners then proceeded on to the Polish church and later attended the final rites in the parish cemetery. Just a few days later the only working mine in the Shenandoah area closed. Immigrant militancy had won a complete victory.

The effects of the East European demonstrations were not confined to Shenandoah alone. The Shenandoah Slavs stimulated fellow immigrants in other communities and terrified other workers. For example, the Mahanoy City workers who had hesitated at the start went out as a result of the Shenandoah riot according to a Reading Company superintendent. There, too, in later incidents the foreigners abused the few who tried to work, and the same intimidation appeared at Mt. Carmel early in October.

It was in late September and early October that the major unrest occurred in Lehigh. One riot especially, the Oneida-Sheppton affair, caused particular union concern. Here the immigrant threat against the Anglo-Saxon officials and workers was more acute and vicious than elsewhere. Even more than in Shenandoah the violence was a patch matter, with women taking a vital role. As a result of a popular mine guard's death, the American community was affected as well.

Through the last week of September several assaults by Slavs, mainly women, resulted in an atmosphere of hostility, and eventually the dynamiting of a boardinghouse reputedly full of Polish nonstrikers forced the union to make its position clear. In a public notice at the beginning of October UMW headquarters declared that such violent acts of "ignorant foreign strikers" caused "President Mitchell and labor leaders some uneasiness." The union, therefore, would not countenance such irresponsible behavior.

The disavowal was timely, for just a week later the most serious incident of the entire strike took place. It of course involved Slavs in the twin hamlets of Sheppton and Oneida, which stand at either side of a road leading into Hazleton. In 1900 these coal towns were forlorn-looking colonies of brownish-black shanties, jerry-built with the usual scrap material and housing almost exclusively Slavic inhabitants, Slovaks and Poles, for the most part Coxe Brothers' employees. The majority of men there in the local union had obeyed the strike call, while a few strays dissented. But when on October 8 a large group of twenty-five from Oneida decided to continue working, trouble resulted. The next day the Sheppton

171

men crossed over to join the loyal Oneida strikers in a noisy demonstration, warning the town's workers to stay home. Early the next morning mobs, including the ubiquitous "Hungarian women," stopped colliery-bound laborers. Some workers refused to go home, and the strikers used force. The escape of thirteen nonstrikers through the picket lines especially antagonized the immigrants, and later a group of men and women armed with clubs and stones assaulted the Oneida breaker itself. They succeeded in driving out the men inside, beating up two company officials, and roughly handling Superintendent L. C. Smith of the DL and W. The latter arrested a striking youth, Joe Prepski, but a Polish mob broke into the place where he was being held, rescued the prisoner, and returned to Oneida in triumph.

Later in the morning the riot reached its climax. Coxe Brothers' Oneida Number 2 had started up and in time attracted five hundred strikers, who lined up facing twenty coal-and-iron police. The mob was largely unorganized until, according to the *Daily Standard,* "a large woman [waving] a club over her head" rallied the foreigners and led a charge. The guards, in dispersing the crowd, discharged their weapons and wounded some immigrant attackers. The strikers gave chase and returned the fire with missiles and bullets of their own. The enraged Slavs eventually caught two policemen, Ralph Mills and George Kellner. A company official later found Mills dead, shot twice in the back, and Kellner unconscious from a head wound.

The resistance had so fired the immigrant settlement

that that evening bands paraded through the streets, with their followers shouting and banging on doors. They again warned against continuing work, and some even marched over to Mills' home at Beaver Meadow where the dead man lay and frightened his widow and four children. By the time Gobin's men had arrived from Shenandoah to restore order, the Oneida casualties had mounted to one dead and thirteen wounded. The English-speaking population was appalled; the authorities hastily arrested eleven "Slavonians" and by January had them convicted and sentenced.

The 1900 strike, then, because of its unprecedented industrywide character, illuminates for the first time why the Slavic miners behaved as they did. The fact that violence stemmed from community rather than individual action points to a sociological motivation. The immigrants' behavior originated in their attitudes and expectations when they migrated, their desire for wealth, and the extent of their progress in obtaining it.

Superficial critics labeled these newcomers "pauper labor" and from their miserable homes and shabby appearance thought them on the verge of starvation. The Pole or Lithuanian, however, was building his nest egg for the future. The very institutions of his life in America, his boardinghouse, his parish, and his mutual aid society were established not just for psychological comfort in an alien world but to help him accumulate income.

Evidence at this time suggests the material achievement of the immigrant in the anthracite area. Even during the work suspension, for example, the Hazleton postmaster told a correspondent that immigrants there sent about fifty thousand dollars per month to Europe. Another report revealed that thrifty Poles already were scaling the economic ladder and building good homes. Still another observer warned not to mistake East European squalor: "Men and women in these rude homes are barefoot, but the merchants will tell you that they do not go without comforts because they are poor. Some of them are becoming wealthy."[29] Mitchell himself thought that the economical living of the Slavs' boardinghouses with their little vegetable gardens and livestock did much to sustain the non-English-speaking mineworker during the contest, and after an anthracite-region tour just before the strike an official of the Nebraska Bureau of Labor and Industrial Statistics marveled at how little the "Hungarians and Poles were suffering despite their poor living conditions."[30]

The powerful drive toward material wealth did not of course mean working at dictated terms. Along with the quest for property was a sense of a worker's dignity —a dignity enforceable only by his ethnic community and its structure. It was that collective organization that more than any other force gave the union victory. Immigrant society compelled conformity in crisis. "The only public opinion they know is the opinion of their neighbors and fellow-workmen. This opinion may be expressed in sullen silence, in shouts of 'scab' . . . or in actual personal violence. However it is expressed, few dare to disregard it."[31] And the same observer added,

174

"Even the women . . . will encourage the men" to strike and demonstrate.

Slavdom's organization also meant rapid communication through all hard-coal patches, another aid in rallying hosts to the strike. Quite likely, for example, immigrant agitators from Mt. Carmel, Centralia, and elsewhere converged on Shenandoah to bring about the militant action. In the manner of a chain reaction other media, such as parades, messengers, and newspapers, spread through the settlements and directed patch opinion. Any transgression of the general will was known quickly, and pressure was applied to any weak point in the form of a demonstration.

Finally, Slavic immigrant rule had an influence beyond its own kind, on victims like O'Hara, policemen like Mills, or Shenandoah Anglo-Saxons. And this may have been the foreigners' most valuable contribution. The "Hungarians" helped to create a prostrike atmosphere among all groups. Through marches, attacks, and threats the foreigners generated a pressure compelling all men to quit work and remain idle.[32]

Of course the Slavs' recognition of labor protest was not entirely the result of a sociological process. The hard work of Fahy, James, and immigrant leaders effectively educated the foreign rank and file to understand what the union was for and the machinery that it offered. Mitchell's charismatic character added another attractive symbol. But essentially more intimate factors conditioned their response, which was to act in concert to win what they had come for. One Lithuanian minister in

175

Freeland predicted his people's feelings in the forthcoming 1900 strike: "If they strike . . . they will strike for good, that is sure. They are hot blooded and if they remain away from work, they will not allow any others, either of their own nationality or English speaking men, to resume unless the union says so."

A short while after the struggle Reverend Peter Roberts described those immigrant traits which led to labor victory: "It was practically a complete tie-up of the anthracite . . . industry and was a great surprise. . . . These foreigners have proved capable of forming labor organizations which are more compact and united than any which ever existed among the various English-speaking nationalities." One indispensable element in the union victory was clear:

> It is conceded by men intimate with the situation throughout the coal fields during the last strike, that its universality was more due to the Sclav than to any other nationality. There would have been, in all probability, a break in the ranks in Schuylkill County had it not been for the firm and uncompromising attitude of the Sclavs in favor of the strike. They have been trained to obedience, and when they organize, they move with an unanimity that is seldom seen among nations who pride themselves on personal liberty and free discussion.[33]

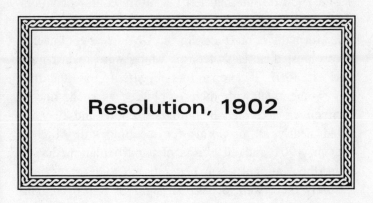

Resolution, 1902

THE HARD-COAL OPERATORS, OF COURSE, BELIEVED THAT
political realities, not labor's power, had forced them to
surrender and offer terms. This was a truce, not a treaty;
they had lost a battle, not a war. The real outcome, the
decision of whether a national union could maintain
itself permanently in the anthracite districts, lay in the
future. In 1901 the mineowners would prepare for another struggle, which eventually began in May, 1902.
When it was over, after five months, operators found
their opponents still there, for the arbitrated decision in
effect established the UMW in the area for good. Once
again, as so often before, the victory stemmed from vigorous action on the part of Mitchell and his subordinates
and, more particularly, on the part of the Slavs. This
1902 contest was to show even more clearly than prior

strikes the particular ethnic reaction of a firmly resolute Slavic community.

The 1900 dispute had left the future course of union-management relations uncertain. The companies had never formally conferred with the UMW leaders but had merely posted notices of terms which were to last until April 1, 1901. The operators repeatedly asserted that they would deal with their employees as such, not as members of a foreign labor organization, and they rejected nearly all proposals for meeting with Mitchell early in 1901 and all efforts of a particular mediating body, the National Civic Federation (NCF).

Surely there were occasional signs of improved relations. The Erie president did confer with Mitchell and indicated that the mineowners might consider a union contract. But the proposal was sterile. With a growing depression wiping out pay gains and friction mounting between union and nonunion workers another strike seemed likely. A rash of petty local disputes plagued the Wyoming and Lehigh areas particularly; over a hundred conflicts took place in the year after the 1900 settlement. When President Thomas refused Mitchell a second conference, hard-coal inhabitants noted operators accumulating inventories and even constructing stockades around their workings. Armageddon was not far off.

However, the "Boy President" as usual worked hard for a settlement, especially by trying to ease the member-nonmember friction. And together with the NCF, Mitchell forced a delay in any union ultimatum, while they prevailed on J. P. Morgan and the operators to negotiate.

By mid-March, 1902, the UMW rank and file were growing impatient. At a tridistrict convention at Shamokin the delegates formulated their final demands, mainly a 20-percent wage increase, an eight-hour day, equitable docking procedures, and a collective bargaining agreement with union recognition.[1] Under pressure from the NCF and Mitchell the union agreed to delay an ultimatum for another month. Mitchell later made even more concessions for peace by reducing the wage demand and postponing any strike-vote session to mid-May. The company presidents, however, still held their position.

At the UMW Hazleton meeting it was clear that the men had delayed long enough. Over Mitchell's opposition the delegates forced the Executive Board to order a temporary suspension of work starting Monday, May 12.[2] The strike was ratified by a relatively close vote on the fourteenth, 461¼ to 349¾. The workers were to remain out on the basis of the Shamokin demands.[3]

The conservatives and Mitchell were able to modify the walkout and salvage some restrictions. Some radicals had wanted a joint meeting with soft-coal members and a general coal strike. The bituminous men were working under their own contract, and Mitchell fought hard and successfully to exclude them from this struggle.

In addition, not all the hard-coal workers were called out. The strike order exempted the maintenance workers, without whom the mines and machinery would have been damaged. Conservatives were able to give the Executive Board discretion in the pullout of these men. Only after the operators rejected the union's eight-hour-

179

day demand for the skilled firemen, pumpmen, and engineers was the suspension authorized for them on June 2. The contest was now all-out economic war.

Strangely enough, as the strike began, few outside the region took any interest. Spring turned to summer, and neither side showed any signs of weakening. In the long, hot days of June and July only an occasional incident reminded the public that the dispute still existed. The novelist Frank Norris, for example, visited some Lehigh patches and marveled at the pervading calm. He depicted the men sitting outside their painted, dilapidated shacks as seemingly on an extended holiday. Norris did notice occasional stirrings: the wind blowing swirls of coal dust, some bedraggled geese scurrying to and fro, and men outside repairing their homes or tinkering in their gardens. Only the new, high board fence topped with barbed wire surrounding the gaunt breaker reminded one of the strike.[4]

However, as fall approached and the temperature dropped, the country naturally began to interest itself in fuel. As September arrived, the two sides were still at a stalemate. Obviously the coming winter necessitated coal reserves for the public, but there were none. Politicians now increasingly demanded action. Mayors, governors, representatives, and senators appealed to and threatened the participants to negotiate. But the operators especially remained adamant. The emerging national crisis required the leading representatives to act.

President Theodore Roosevelt was very much concerned by September. After soliciting advice from many quarters, the Chief Executive decided to invite the combatants to an unprecedented conference with him in Washington. This meeting proved fruitless, and public hysteria over the lack of fuel grew. The President at this point was desperate enough to consider working the mines with troops. However, his friend, Elihu Root, then Secretary of War, convinced J. P. Morgan to press his anthracite colleagues to accept arbitration. After some hesitation both sides agreed to the personnel on the arbitrating commission. At a Wilkes-Barre convention on October 20 the mineworkers agreed to return to work on the twenty-third.

So the greatest strike in the area to that time was over. Having tied up an entire industry for 165 days, a longer period than anyone, including their leader, might have predicted, about one hundred thousand mineworkers now marched back to the pits. Most of the men reoiled their tools and resumed their labors gladly.[5]

The long suspension had been a great feat for the young labor organization. While the unionists did not know what sort of a victory they had won, in contrast to events in earlier stoppages a labor body had at least survived very much intact after five months of economic privation. Also, the result was arbitration, something which Mitchell had proposed at the start of the contest, but which the operators had consistently refused. The huge loss in wages had not weakened rank-and-file unity, and UMW morale seemed as high as ever.

UMW organizational procedures played an educational role in developing union sentiment among all workers. Union leaders had continued to recognize and foster immigrant participation in labor association ever since the 1900 strike; the Fahy strategy of encouraging and sponsoring Slavic affiliation with a light hand was maintained in all districts. For example, just after the 1900 contest one immigrant-UMW intermediary, Frank Petosky, wrote to his countrymen in the *Journal* to join the organization. He also urged his fellows to get "your father or brother or friend [as he] comes from the old country [and] make a union man out of him. [For] we will get along nicely and smoothly in this country then."[6]

The UMW's greatest talent in dealing with the newer nationalities lay in the choice of men as leaders—men already high in group esteem. The *Journal*'s business agent was such a leader. This figure, Louis Hammerling, perhaps more by guile than merit, paradoxically had a high reputation among the area's East Europeans.[7] He was founder and general manager of the Lithuanian-Polish Club of Luzerne County, a very popular educational organization which helped Slavs gain citizenship and incidentally published propaganda for labor. Through 1901 one of its projects was soliciting contributions for a monument to the Lattimer victims, although the effort was unsuccessful.

To further attract the immigrants, each district followed Fahy's policy of granting the Slavs high office in its councils. The vice-presidency of every district consistently was reserved for them. Through 1900, 1901, and 1902, District 9 honored Paul Pulaski with that position, and he continued his tireless missionary activity throughout the anthracite area. Lehigh chose the German Pole, Anthony Schlosser, who had thoroughly earned his office by having probably done more work there in 1901 among immigrants than any other foreign-born organizer. When he stepped down in 1902, the men selected another Slav, Andrew Matti of Hazleton.

Wyoming had more difficulty in finding a good foreign representative. Here Slavs were more suspicious of the older nationalities ever since Anglo-Saxons had criticized immigrant violence in the 1899 Susquehanna and 1900 strikes. Yet finally delegates to the 1901 District 1 convention did find a popular Lithuanian, Adam Ryscavage of Plymouth, for the position. They reelected him vice-president in 1902 and 1903. The prolabor *Straż* applauded the UMW's recognition of Poles (calling the Wyoming vice-president "Ryskiewicz," a Pole) and praised the work of the three vice-presidents as a compliment to their nationality, and the 1902 Shamokin convention chose the three immigrant officeholders to help erect a fitting memorial to the Lattimer victims.

Thus before the major 1902 strike the UMW hierarchy allowed the aliens considerable representation. Once the suspension began, the leaders were to reap their reward. For the response of the immigrants was again almost universally prounion, and, as had happened before, their action disciplined the entire work force.

The first alien reaction was similar to that of 1888 and 1900, only on a grander scale. Many East Europeans simply left the region, some cutting their ties permanently and others sending back to those left behind enough income to continue the struggle. The exodus started early. So-called "Johnny Mitchell specials" going westward gathered the "Hungarian" bachelors and breadwinners from numerous anthracite hamlets and deposited them in the Pennsylvania or Virginia bituminous fields.[8] Others went east. As a traveler put it, "The unmarried Hungarians and Poles . . . had nearly all money saved ahead, and many . . . had already set out for New York, Philadelphia, and other cities to get work as unskilled laborers, while the strike lasted."[9] Only a fortnight after May 12 about two thousand had already left Shenandoah. The total emigration was surprisingly large, about one-third of the 147,000 in the work force.[10] In fact, so many East Europeans withdrew savings deposits to wait out the suspension elsewhere that an unusual minor run on the banks resulted.

A second feature of the Slavs on strike was an extension of their normal living habit, an astounding providence. Their thrift and economy proved essential in feeding those left behind. The immigrants' ability to live just above subsistence and to maintain themselves so long without visible income dumbfounded Anglo-Saxons. Support came from fellow countrymen employed far and wide, but many merely cut expenses further and drew on their vast reserves.

Paul Pulaski described one important instrument that kept costs down—the cooperative. He examined three Mt. Carmel groceries run by immigrant locals and found them in good condition. He also described eleven western Schuylkill locals that had healthy treasuries. The district official concluded: "The foreign element . . . can stick this strike out until New Year's, if necessary. . . . They are in a better position . . . to remain on strike for a longer period of time than most of their English speaking neighbors."[11] Time would prove his claims. The records of Polish Local 561 and later findings tended to bear him out.[12]

The East Europeans had already devised other, ingenious ways for saving money. Superficial accounts of their slovenly way of life could not probe their success. The pile of culm, for example, outside the Slav's door provided one means of support. Mineworkers and their families combed the mound for coal, loaded it into wagons, and peddled it in the larger cities. Although the companies sometimes arrested such scavengers for trespassing, the practice continued; and now, during the strike, the Slavic male accompanied his wife in her periodic forays to the dumps.

Huckleberries offered additional profit. Of course, fruit could not suffice entirely as the fare for a boardinghouse full of Slavs. But its harvest could bring another income, since the value of the trade was surprising. As the summer drew on, the berries grew abundantly on the mountains surrounding the region, and the immigrants walked miles to pick them from the thickets. The Mt. Carmel *Daily News* announced that by July one shipper in west Schuylkill was sending out as many as fifteen hundred quarts a day and a month later had sold forty thousand

185

boxes after buying them at five cents each. The price was low, but the income was of great value and provided necessities in many homes. A short time later a Wyoming traveler estimated that a large family could make as much as five dollars a day picking berries.

The economical foreigner also made use of his more traditional sources. Again, as in 1900, he was grateful for his agrarian background. The Slav now cultivated the patch vegetable garden even more assiduously and carefully tended his chickens and livestock.

In 1902, more than in any other contest, the children were a valued asset. Many continued to work in various factories and contribute to the family chest. When the troops arrived in the field, they especially noticed Polish and Lithuanian urchins hanging around their camps, doing odd jobs or panhandling while older adolescents sold carved coal trinkets to the guardsmen.

Finally, every family cut down on their ordinary expenses. Few paid church or societies' dues, and they demanded and received much credit from stores. Most landlords and coal companies usually did not bother to try to collect rent, since no tenant could pay it.

During this strike the comparative economic circumstance of Slav and Anglo-Saxon stood out more sharply than ever. Clearly the newer nationalities appeared the stronger. In a letter to *Straż* in July the "Strikers from Nanticoke" bragged, "We Poles can perhaps remain in an unemployed state longer than our mineworking colleagues of other nationalities." And many observers agreed.

186

Two newspaper correspondents undertook to gauge closely the conditions of unemployment in the average East European patch. One surveyed Shenandoah in the middle of the summer, asking how the Slav could exist. "The only answer I can get to my questions . . . is, 'Oh, they have saved up money.' . . . My guide . . . insisted, as others with whom I talked have done, that . . . the Poles, Hungarians and Lithuanians . . . can live on very little. . . . Though they may not earn much, they save a great deal."[13] An irate Schuylkill storekeeper, a leading merchant who dealt with the foreigners, had an unusual complaint for this interviewer. The Slavs caused him trouble because they had *too much* money. Lithuanians, Polanders, and Huns rarely asked for credit but instead would lay down a twenty-dollar bill for a fifty- or sixty-cent purchase, "thus keeping him constantly short of change."

The other reporter learned that, just as in the hard times of the 1890's, in this difficult period Slavs were still buying land. One of the "more intelligent type" took the visitor on a tour of his property and commented: "Me work at [Cranberry] breaker. I belong to union and won't go back yet. In no hurry for you see me got plenty to do here just now. Feels good to own home like dis. Wife likes it and children too." The correspondent later learned and marveled that at least forty others had cleared land and were spending their idle time digging foundations.[14] He felt that communal cooperation was the main reason for the achievement.

This stress on frugality for the most part aided the

187

strikers' cause. But its intensity was such that on occasion some Slavs objected to the union's relief system. Briefly, since the union based payments on need, the more provident Slav received less than the Anglo-Saxon. The immigrants misunderstood the principle of relief and thought handouts should substitute for normal income, and Slavic objections resulted. The unrest was not general, however, and did not affect the strike.[15]

Certainly observers, especially coal operators, expected a collapse in the strikers' ranks long before the autumn. Even if the Slav could exist longer in his abstinence, they thought that the Anglo-Saxon would refuse to join him and would begin to return to work. But figures show that very few workers of any nationality violated the union directive throughout. Though strike sentiment among the men was far from unanimous, only a few hundred disobeyed the order of May 12. And after the maintenance men joined the strike, 95 percent of the work force stayed out to the end. The total number on the job during the contest never was large:

Number of Employed Anthracite Mineworkers, 1902[16]

April	117,707 (last normal month)	August	7,706
May	56,166	September	8,236
June	16,353	October	36,469
July	6,552	(settled	
		October 23)	

Again, as so often since 1888, the Slavic community character was the backbone of the resistance. The nearly unanimous refusal to return can be attributed to the determined, almost fanatical, immigrant sentiment. Although only rare incidents in the dispute on the local level attracted attention, the "Hungarian" settlements were the most belligerent.

The earliest rumors of immigrant aggression centered in Lehigh. It cannot be stressed enough that throughout the strike, talk of any working laborers before the simple but anxious "hunky" was like waving a red flag before a bull. It was beyond his comprehension why maintenance men should continue at their posts when all had decided for a strike; for him there was no compromise with unity. At Tamaqua, where mines had closed before the start of the contest, the "foreign element" insulted pumpmen who were protecting the mines against flooding, although no violence resulted at first.

The situation grew more serious elsewhere just after the first call out. "Foreigners" at Shenandoah and Park Place (near Mahanoy City) blocked the roads and refused to allow maintenance men to reach their jobs. The Tamaqua immigrants now followed suit. Union officials and interpreters rushed to these areas and tried to reason with the Slavs. Apparently the explanations did not suffice, for on May 17 the *Wilkes-Barre Times* reported that on the day before strikers of "the foreign element . . . commenced to throw missiles" at some firemen at Number 4 near Lansford.

Fearful stories now circulated of a possible general immigrant attack on maintenance men. The metropolitan papers described foreigners hoarding arms and ammunition and secretly drilling for an insurrection. Anthony Schlosser, the District 7 vice-president and spokesman for

189

his countrymen, indignantly denied such rumors: "The foreigners . . . are peaceably inclined."[17] The events of the next five months would decidedly contradict him.

On the whole, however, through June and part of July a remarkable quiet hung over the districts. Strangely, the unrest at that time took place outside the anthracite region; labor sympathizers in Baltimore, New York, and elsewhere objected to the coal companies' recruiting the hated coal-and-iron police along with the needed maintenance engineers. As these hired groups entered the region and took their positions at the barricades, however, they stimulated the Slavic "guards." In late July the peace was broken; a major riot jarred the nation. For a third time in the past fifteen years the violence was at Shenandoah and the agitators Slavic.

Like others who continued at their jobs, Foreman David Landerman and his son had lived behind the enclosure at the Kohinoor Mine all week. Every Sunday they went home to visit their families and return inside the barricade on Monday. But strikers had begun to intercept nonunion men and urge them to keep away from work. To avoid a disturbance, the two men had decided to sneak to work disguised in women's clothes. But a score of strikers recognized them in spite of their costumes and, chasing the two men home, surrounded their house. When the elder Landerman threatened his pursuers with a weapon, a shotgun blast from the crowd wounded him forthwith. The next day the strikers' anger mounted; a group marched on the West Shenandoah Mine and forced it to cease operation, while the tension came to a climax on the thirtieth.

On that day Deputy Sheriff Thomas Beddal was escorting three machinists, Good, Vaughn, and Bennett, from the Reading's Shenandoah City Mine to their homes after work. When the party got to the Reading station, a group of foreigners asked them where they were going and demanded to see the contents of the bundles they were carrying. The trio refused, but the strikers grabbed the parcels and, as they had suspected, found the contents to be working clothes. A fight broke out; two machinists were able to escape, but Beddal and the other machinist fled into the depot, while they shot several attackers on the way. The two men locked themselves in, but the howling mob, now numbering about two thousand and including women and children, began hurling missiles through the windows.

In the meantime the Sheriff's wife begged her brother-in-law, Joseph Beddal, a hardware merchant, to hurry to the station to her husband's aid. The merchant assented and took along some of his clerks to assist. As Joseph Beddal arrived, one of the mob shouted that he was bringing ammunition to free the men inside, and the crowd ferociously turned on him. "He was knocked down and . . . soon tossed around like a ball by the infuriated . . . foreigners who acted like demons instead of human beings."[18] A kindly Lithuanian finally pulled Joseph Beddal, dazed and bloody, from the melee and sent him to a nearby hotel to dress his wounds.

The eight-man Shenandoah police force now appeared, but the throng refused to disperse. Chief Fry finally cleared a path to a train for the besieged inmates, and Thomas Beddal managed to hop onto a car. Although some of the crowd warned the engineer not to work up steam, he did, nevertheless, and the rest of the police, firing as they went, ran to board the engine. But the crowd resumed their stone throwing and caught and beat up one officer, Lauraitis, who had slipped from the moving train. When a bystander tried to rescue the bruised policeman, one of the mob cried, "You son of a b---h, what you pick that man up for—we no kill him, just smash him a bit."[19] Besides Lauraitis, four other officers including Chief Fry had suffered injuries. After the train left, the incensed strikers attacked a Polish priest who had attempted to pacify them.[20] Later that evening the Schuylkill County sheriff arrived with a posse from Pottsville and finally restored order.

The more peaceful inhabitants breathed more easily when the authorities were again in control, but the damage in casualties had been heavy. Over a score were seriously injured, and fifty others hurt, in the day's outburst. The sheriff feared still more rioting and asked the Governor for help. Governor Stone hesitated but, upon receiving another telegram from prominent citizens, sent in fifteen hundred militia under the indomitable Brigadier J. P. S. Gobin. By the thirty-first, Columbia Park again bristled with military tents.

Once the presence of troops had assured the "better element" that no recurrence would take place, a wave of indignation against the Slav swept through the town, for Joseph Beddal, a prominent community figure, had died of his injuries at the Ashland State Hospital. Everyone believed the murderers to have been Lithuanians or, more generally, Slavic immigrants, from the names of the injured rioters: Dolski, Luskus, Wakavage, Savinkus, Binkunas, Belliski, and Pomewicz. Thomas Beddal later confirmed those suspicions by naming Anthony Klimowitz, Stanislaus Zukowski, and Waldo Rowinski as leaders of the mob. The authorities arrested the trio, although the first two denied their guilt. The Colorado Springs *Telegraph* reacted much as did other newspapers: "It was not to be expected that violence could much longer be avoided. The Polacks and Hungarians . . . these hotheaded foreigners do not see why they should not go to all lengths in defending what they regard as their rights."[21] Even the normally sympathetic *Straż* tried to disassociate the Poles from the actual culprits. It berated the Lithuanian strikers soundly and warned that such happenings could lead to another Lattimer Massacre. A Lithuanian fraternal order in Shenandoah admitted ethnic responsibility but answered critics by claiming that other nationalities took part in the disturbance, too.

On the other hand, civic-minded persons praised the English-speaking worker for his passivity and good sense. A National Guard officer separated strikers by ethnic origins: "The Lithuanians fear neither man nor God. They have no regard for law or order or anything. . . . The English speaking miners are all right and had done a great deal to help the troops."[22] The indictment of two Lithuanians, a one-armed saloonkeeper and a butcher, for Beddal's murder went far to satisfy the American community.

Of course the UMW leaders acted quickly to discountenance the riot. District President Fahy immediately posted notices in the surrounding hamlets announcing that the outbreaks were contrary to the explicit instructions of the union leaders. Mitchell, too, lost no time in emphatically condemning any lawlessness. A few days later Shenandoah unionists won popular approval by denouncing a Slavic attack on a town barber who serviced the militia.

Despite rumors of more serious unrest to come, the Shenandoah Slavs did not resume their attacks, probably because of the presence of soldiers. Nevertheless this original riot of July 30 served to stimulate agitators in other towns; Poles and Lithuanians bombed the homes of a fire boss in Gilberton and a guard in Minersville. And by late September the Mt. Carmel newspaper was tiring of minor incidents there: "Again . . . was the good name of our city disgraced by . . . crowds of hoodlums [and] the Poles, by far, comprise the largest part of these mobs."[23]

Lehigh was the most peaceful district, but foreigners here, too, used Shenandoah as an example. The day after the Beddal incident the *Daily Standard* blared forth the headline LANSFORD IN TURMOIL; five hundred strikers, "mostly foreigners," had made war on two hundred Lehigh Coal and Navigation Company shophands going to work. Similar assaults by "mostly foreigners" took place against scabs in Summit Hill and Tamaqua.

The arrival of Gobin's troops finally restored order to the southern regions in September. But of course the third district, Wyoming, was still unpoliced—except by the Slavic "troops." Once again only state protection could immobilize the immigrant enthusiasts.

It is unnecessary to enumerate here the confrontations in the north of Slavic-led mob and scabs. The only peculiar feature of these incidents was the greater role of Slavic women, some pursuing strikebreakers on marches even with babes in arms. Particularly shocking was the brutal death of a scab, James Winston, at Olyphant, but responsibility of the Slavs for the murder, although implied, was never proven.

Non-Slavic reaction to these constant incidents ranged from serious concern to outright hysteria. Both UMW leadership and its Anglo-Saxon membership always disassociated the union from this violence. They recognized that the immigrant militancy was on behalf of the strike, but they earnestly condemned the foreigners' means. In the midst of the Wyoming attacks Mitchell sent in Martin Menolo, an Italian, and Anthony Schlosser, the Pole, to lead "peace committees" to convince the immigrants that they were injuring their cause by violence.

All available evidence indicates that every facility and institution of the Slavic neighborhood was directed toward strike support. Especially colorful in 1902 were the efforts of the Slavs' musical organizations on behalf of the strikers. Music and dancing had played an important part in the Old World folkways, and parishes had continued this tradition in America. Two local bands, one from Mt. Carmel and the other from Shenandoah, became particularly noteworthy on tour. They educated the public at large and collected funds for the strikers.

The Mt. Carmel group, affiliated with St. Joseph's Polish Roman Catholic Church, left the coal fields in the fall, visited nearby localities, and solicited contributions. The other group, Shenandoah's Lithuanian Band, attracted more widespread attention. In September it traveled through New Jersey and Brooklyn to play in parks and at public events and ask for donations. By October the group had sent home over three thousand dollars.

More effective than the money-making activity of communal organizations to extend prostrike sentiment was the quick and sure punishment meted out to nonconformists. The result of such enforcement was a wide-ranging intimidation. *Straż* caught the feeling in mid-June: "The ranks of the Polish scabs in the last few days have lessened considerably. Coercive rocks and a couple of broken ribs have influenced them—for strikers caught some traitors to the workers' cause and so licked them that they will remember it for a long time."

The Shenandoah incident created a warlike atmosphere throughout the Schuylkill area. The *Ashland Advocate* complained in August, "Now no man dare assert in public anything but intense loyalty to the union," and there *was* tangible proof for the contention that immigrant war was near: some Polish military fraternals were holding more frequent drills.

The immigrant community made the working nonstriker of their own nationality very uncomfortable. He

196

was harassed, persecuted, and even ostracized. A John Luksic worked in a DL and W breaker for ten days until pressure from his neighbors, Gernofsky and Vallakonski, forced him to quit. Another antiunion Pole, Thomas Szanisky, suffered humiliation at his wedding, being forced to confess his sin to his comrades on bended knee.

Perhaps the most significant indication of Slavic pro-strike opinion was the aid given by the fraternal orders, the organizations upon which the East European based his security. On the national level the National Slovak Society pledged its fifty-thousand-dollar surplus for its five thousand members in the strike districts in case of hardship, and the Chicago Sokols agreed to take up collections there. Within the coal region local fraternal branches punished scabbing members. Lawrence Twardoski testified that after a mob had killed his ducks and taken his cow, both the St. Joseph's Society and the Polish National Alliance expelled him. And also in the Hazleton region the *Plain Speaker* reported early in the strike: "Many of the foreign societies . . . adopted resolutions expelling those members who have refused to strike." Elsewhere the societies at least fined transgressors.[24]

The regular communication channels, the immigrant newspapers, strengthened Slavic unity and contributed to community sentiment in support of the strike. Both *Gornik* and *Straż* reminded their readers that the public sympathized with them and awaited their forthcoming victory.[25] *Slovak v Amerike* warned its people to beware of any traitors who might try to mislead the strikers.

197

The Slavic Community on Strike

That warning was a response to a new technique that employers were using for the first time to divide the strikers' ranks. Some understood the locus of labor determination and recognized that the best chance of breaking the strike lay in creating dissension between foreigners and natives. Their failure to weaken the immigrant resolve attests to its durability.

For example, just after the strike started, a letter of May 16 in the *Scranton Times* announced that "the Polish, Slavish and Lithuanian men do not wish, nor intend to strike"; the signers were a "Committee of Laborers" named Resenitz, Worsznar, and Mesheskie. But a few days later the paper reported: "If there ever existed any doubt as to loyalty of Polish mine workers to the United Mine Workers of America it was dispelled at a meeting of over 600," where the "stray sheep" who wrote the letter were denounced. The meeting then pledged full devotion to Schlosser and Mitchell.

A few days later businessmen of Panther Creek Valley attempted to induce immigrant helpers to go back to work for miners who had already signified their intention to continue on the job. Apparently they had no more success than a group of operator-sponsored organizers who tried to form an independent Slavic union.

In the middle of June several coal-and-iron police tried to persuade the inhabitants of a Polish settlement near Plymouth to return to work, but the police were beaten and chased out of town. Recruiters of immigrant scabs in the West Virginia soft-coal strike then going on received the same treatment.

By October the operators grew desperate. Some companies offered bribes to various local presidents if they could arouse a general back-to-work movement.[26] Adam Ryscavage, District 1 vice-president, warned his countrymen with apparent success to beware of such tricks. The advice came none too soon, for the following week a German language circular, which attempted to divide the Slavs from their Irish union leaders, was passed among the strikers. It urged East Europeans to "act . . . for your countrymen and families. . . . The Irish are always capable of turning against you. . . . Act at once and for yourself . . . A FRIEND." But the effort even that late found the foreign ranks as solid as ever. The years of work of Mitchell, Fahy, Pulaski, Schlosser, and others had too well cemented the nationalities.

Besides the physical and moral coercion of the Slavic community a final, less tangible factor contributed to that element's unified support, the members' identification with their leader, John Mitchell. In 1900 and even 1901 East Europeans had admired their handsome union president. But with the expansion of the 1902 contest the Slav raised the "Young Old Man" to nearly divine status.

Why Mitchell was so much adored is conjectural. Certainly his own taciturn conservatism, his poise, and his religious demeanor contributed to his exalted position. Essential, however, in this contest was his unique ability to acquire and retain public confidence. While Pulaski, Schlosser, and Ryscavage represented the immigrant in the union, Mitchell spoke well for their cause to the United States and to the President, and also to the employers.

According to one of Mitchell's closest aides the esteem

199

of the foreigners for the man was enormous. "To a great many of the newly arrived miners John Mitchell is the one great man in the United States. Possibly they have heard of Pierpont Morgan and they had a dim idea there is such a man as President Roosevelt, but ask the first Hun or Polander on the streets who is president of the United States and the odds are about even he will reply, 'Johnny D'Mitch.' "[27] And a son of one foreign miner stated that almost every anthracite Slav hung Johnny Mitchell's picture on his wall beside those of his saints.

In fact, from the immigrants' worm's-eye view, the whole dispute at the industrial and national level was like an allegory. When the operators insulted the UMW head in Washington, all mineworkers' hearts warmed to their leader as to a hero in the midst of villains. Like children, they watched the unfolding drama with fascination.

Strangely enough, Mitchell himself could not fathom the Slavic reverence toward him. The UMW President described an illustrative episode that took place during the struggle. Arriving at a predominantly immigrant town, Mitchell encountered an immense crowd of about fifty thousand men, women, and children who met his train at the station. A cordon of police had to conduct Mitchell's carriage through the throng. The labor leader noticed that "many of the foreign workmen instead of being interested in the parade seemed to be eyeing the policemen suspiciously and . . . I observed many of them producing revolvers and cudgels. I made inquiry of some of the English speaking men as to the meaning of this demonstration, and was told that the foreigners . . . feared that the policemen might do me injury and they felt it incumbent on themselves to protect me." In a later passage he said: "I could see that a considerable number of these foreign workmen had stationed themselves at points from which they could watch my hotel; and in the morning when I awoke, I could see . . . some of the men . . . still standing guard to see no harm came to me."[28]

The greatest tribute of Pole, Lithuanian, Slovak, and Ukrainian to their chief came at the end of the strike. In late October the anthracite people gave vent to their relief and joy. The ordeal had ended and families again would have normal incomes. Even though the final decision would not come for several more months, immigrants and their fellow workers celebrated the victory with parades. They revered John Mitchell as the individual who had guided them through the long battle and sought to demonstrate their feeling in a testimonial.

The ceremony took place in the main hall of Wilkes-Barre's Hotel Hart on October 26. On stage were Mitchell, the three district leaders, certain local officials, and the chief Slavic labor organizer, Paul Pulaski, who read the eulogy. The style may have been somewhat pompous and labored, but no one doubted its sincerity:

> Mr. President—We, the undersigned committee representing the anthracite coal region, of Polish, Ruthenian, Lithuanian and Slavic descent, feeling the most sincere appreciation and deepest gratitude for your manly, energetic, disinterested, self-sacrificing and vigorous conducting of the last anthracite

201

strike . . . do hereby express our most sincere thanks for protecting our interests and for the hard struggle you undertook for us.

Blessed be the moment when you, as salvator of our troubles . . . arrived in our midst and . . . boldly and courageously stood like a hero against . . . adverses.

But nothing could withstand your ingenious leadership, a second Napoleon of labor, your every step was a conquest and a victory.

Receive, dear leader, a thousand-fold blessing of all the poor, hard working and struggling people, who shall teach their children, that the embodiment of everything that is pure, just, right and sublime is our president, John Mitchell.

The paper was signed by the editors of four foreign-language newspapers; Joseph Lindsay, Paul Pulaski, Anthony Schlosser, and three other Slavs signed it for the immigrant union members; and at least five laymen, including Louis Hammerling and John Nemeth, affixed their names "for the Citizens."

Pulaski then presented Mitchell a one-hundred-dollar gold watch and an elaborate two-hundred-fifty-dollar gold medallion which resembled the emancipation badge that freed slaves had given Lincoln. On the top bar were the initials "J. M." set in diamonds, and below were the UMW insignia and a miner's pick and shovel crossed above a mine lamp. The inscription read, "Presented to John Mitchell, president of United Mine Workers of America, from the Polish, Lithuanian and Slavonian people of the anthracite coal fields of Pennsylvania."

Another speaker told of a projected solicitation among Poles and Lithuanians to raise a huge sum (one hundred thousand dollars) for their leader. Characteristically the man of the hour then arose and quietly thanked Pulaski and "his people" in a brief reply. He also begged his well-wishers to avoid any financial gift which might separate him from the rank and file.

Three days later was Mitchell Day, and in still another tribute to their President the mineworkers went wild with enthusiasm. About nine-tenths of the work force took a holiday; some stores and schools closed for the celebration, and most communities held parades.[29]

Of course the strikers were celebrating prematurely. Only when the newly formed Anthracite Commission gave its decision could one judge how truly successful were Mitchell's leadership and the determination of the Slavs. The presidential tribunal might very well negate all of the union demands.

After the Commission members visited the anthracite region, the interested sides prepared their briefs for the hearings.[30] The noted attorney Clarence Darrow, along with H. D. Lloyd, Mitchell, and aides, presented the union's case, while the operators' lawyers called the UMW a disruptive influence. After a long parade of 558 witnesses and ten thousand pages of testimony, the hearings ended on February 5, 1903.

The Commission's findings appeared in mid-March. In terms of the original Shamokin demands the award gave to the mineworkers generally and the union in particular almost everything they had demanded. Where the union had demanded a 20 percent wage increase (but later reduced it to 10), the award granted 10 percent to nearly everyone: contract miners, maintenance men, and company hands, excepting only some engineers and pumpmen. Where the union had demanded equitable weight measurement for men paid by the carload, the award stated that the 1875 statute already allowed the men a checkweighman and should be enforced. Where the union had demanded a 20 percent decrease in hours, the award ordered substantially a 10 percent decrease. As for the other grievances, the award merely condemned company houses and other forms of compulsion, favoritism, and discrimination.

The most sensitive issue to the union was the demand for recognition. By not granting this request on the ground that it was beyond the scope of its authority the Commission did hurt the labor organization. The tribunal did, however, go far in that direction through the establishment of continuing grievance machinery, the Anthracite Board of Conciliation. This board consisted of three representatives of the majority of the workers and three of the companies, who were to consider individual disputes as they arose. If that body was unable to agree, the third Federal circuit court would appoint an umpire. One could say that the Board did allow partial UMW recognition in that the "representatives of the majority of the mineworkers" on the panel were and have continued to be the three union district presidents.

Again, while the award did not grant formal recognition, it contributed materially to collective bargaining by offering operators an institutionalized acquaintance with labor organization; the precedent of meetings between union leaders and management to consider grievances had been set, and both sides had now accepted a large measure of industrial democracy.

The essential achievement, then, of the 1902 strike was making the union secure in the hard-coal region, and it was the Slavic nationalities who contributed most to that success. As savers they had accumulated an amazing reserve; as immigrants they had created a viable community; and as workers they used that communal structure in support of the strike.

As an epilogue to the drama, attorney Clarence Darrow offered his explanation of why the East Europeans behaved as they did. In a stirring summation before the Anthracite Commission, he pleaded for understanding and forbearance of peasant-immigrant violence:

> They tell us that [union enthusiasts] were cruel. Were [they?] I will not [lay] any [such description] upon the poor, stuttering Pole . . . a warm-hearted sympathetic, emotional, religious people, living close to the heart of nature, and feeling her every pulse-beat —these men are the peers in courage, in devotion, in conscience of any man who lives. The evidence in this case may show that they the more often overstepped the law. It may. But there is the law of the land and there is the moral law. . . . No man has the moral right—whatever the legal right may be . . . to work when that work interferes with the . . . living relations of his fellow man. . . . The scab is a man who . . . always has been hated [and] always will be hated.[31]

205

X

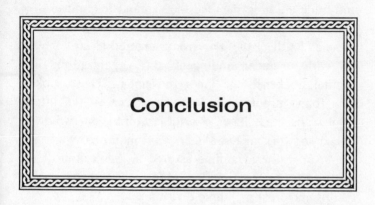

Conclusion

DURING THE 1870'S AND 1880'S THE ORIGINS OF NEW-comers entering the United States began to shift. At first Americans welcomed these newer peoples with strange customs and incomprehensible tongues. Most citizens, themselves descendants of immigrants, believed in the symbol of this nation as a haven for the oppressed as it is described in Emma Lazarus' famous poem. But as these foreign entrants increased further and piled into American cities, farms, and industrial centers to recon-struct their Old World institutions, some began to doubt the wisdom of the traditional unrestricted immigration. With a mixture of xenophobia and uncertainty about the effect of such aliens on American values, the citi-zenry became concerned. They reasoned that the influx would affect the present society adversely, and if the economic results were detrimental to the American way of life, perhaps the gates should be closed. Nativists, patriots, and trade union leaders led the demand for reform.

Union advocates especially complained about the newcomers. To them the new groups entered as strikebreakers, with no understanding of labor organization; their coming weakened the labor movement. These spokesmen found proof in the popular stories of the utterly helpless, destitute Slavic peasant just off the boat who was forced to work at sub-American conditions, while the employer in the meantime assured his subjection of the work force by continually bringing in other national groups and creating ethnic division.

John R. Commons expressed such fears of the foreigner at the turn of the century. He found recent aliens

> unfamiliar with the traditions and customs of [labor] organization, unaccustomed to the rules and control which it imposes, incapable of [unionizing] through their ignorance of the language, and, moreover, forced by their poverty to work for low wages, and, by their lack of friends to work with docility and desperate energy for him who first gives [them] a job. . . . The constant influx of immigrants into a trade nullifies . . . the educational work of organization almost as rapidly as it is conducted.[1]

Other authorities charged that the new nationalities "who are often willing to work for low wages and who fail to appreciate the benefit of organization, have all interfered with the permanence of unions."[2] One expert pointed to the Poles specifically and called them "very

208

poor unionists . . . much more successful as strike breakers than union members," and, another added, the Polish nationality won that mark as "their racial opprobrium."[3]

Early in 1907 an aroused Congress authorized a commission led by Senator William Dillingham of Vermont to examine the impact of unrestricted immigration on American life. The investigation seemed thorough; the effort cost about eight hundred thousand dollars, took over three years to complete, and produced a report totaling forty-two volumes. The study merely reiterated the current feeling about the newer immigrants. It found that the southern and eastern Europeans were unstable in their industrial relations, would not strike, and tended to demoralize labor organizations.

So restrictionists now could call on a lengthy government document to support their contentions. And more recent studies still accept all or part of the commission's conclusions on immigrants and unions:

> Undoubtedly, the successive waves of immigration retarded the progress of organized labor. It was not only the fact that during their first years in America the immigrants were engaged in ceaseless and hard work, and absorbed in orienting themselves in a new environment that made foreign-born communities stony soil for sowing the gospel of unionism, but also the fact that employers capitalized [on] the divisions among wage earners along nationalistic, racial and religious lines.[4]

The latest historical opinion continues with some am-

209

bivalence to view early Slavic American settlements as disorganized and weak particularly during industrial unrest. One scholar has concluded that the long non-union era in steel was in part due to the new nationalities' social structure, which reflected considerable insecurity, mobility, and thus instability. The ex-peasants, then, were clearly "unpromising union material."[5] However, these findings came from the views of English language observers of immigrant living conditions and, as the historian himself concedes, apply only to the early years. He agrees that by the early 1900's Slavic communities did support unionization. Dissent at that time was dangerous; a group member "could not conceive of differing with group decisions."[6] Nevertheless, a recent account of the Homestead Strike implies that immigrants demonstrated labor loyalty even then, in the early 1890's.[7]

Certainly the actions of the Slavs in the anthracite area, then, suggest a modification in the established view of immigrants as strikebreakers or docile union destroyers. Such an assertion overlooks certain basic developments in the newcomers' living pattern in America. Above all, one should remember that for the East European immigrant his American world, where he settled, lived, worked, and even died, was his parish or patch; he had built it himself to provide every possible element necessary for ethnic comfort. It was a substantial achievement.

The Slav hardly arrived alone, lost, uprooted, disoriented "with a lack of friends." To the contrary, letters from relatives and friends in the already developed immigrant community brought him here, and members of

210

that community greeted him on arrival and got him a job. It was as a part of the community that he labored in the breaker or mine, and it was within that immigrant society that he developed attitudes toward striking and unionism. These attitudes, then, stemmed from the three major characteristics of all immigrant Slavs: their quest for income, their ability to economize, and their close group attachment. It was these impulses that compelled them to assert or support group sentiment forcefully in times of labor crisis.

Hard-coal history to 1903 proves that cohesive elements of East European society, Polish, Lithuanian, Slovak, and Ruthenian, caused its members to carry on the workers' cause resolutely and tolerate no dissension. Once the community approved of the strike, it demanded conformity of its members. Few dared trangress that local judgment, for the Slav's cultural identity was at stake. The ethnic communities had been created to fill a need for security, and the descriptions of these groups are filled with such terms as "solidarity," "religious devotion," "crusade," and "loyalty." The result of such cohesion was the secure establishment of the labor union in the anthracite districts.[8]

Thus it is chimerical to ascribe the delay in unionization to the Slavs. Before the 1890's the East European immigrants had little or nothing to do with unionism's struggle. Hard times, the power of operators, incomplete organization, and defective and conservative leadership killed the WBA, the Amalgamated, and the Knights; and northeastern Pennsylvania hardly noticed the new nationalities before the early 1880's. When by 1885 Slavic communities were forming in the region, the AA and the Knights at the same time were building their organizations there: one can hardly attribute their demise to the Slavic mineworker. On the contrary, the vital 1887–1888 struggle showed that East European activity when it erupted tried to save the unions and the strike, not destroy them. But labor leaders were apparently too busy quarreling over internal strategy to recognize, utilize, and direct this reservoir of support.

The Lattimer Massacre was an important lesson to John Fahy and the other union leaders, for it proved the weakness of restrictionist politicking and the strength of the immigrants' determination in strikes. After this, Fahy would accurately assess the anthracite region's social and demographic composition and establish guidelines for later organizers to follow. His efforts and the projected image of President Mitchell assured Slavic loyalty to the union, which in turn yielded invaluable dividends in 1900 and 1902; for without the immigrants' powers of cohesion, resistance, and militancy the UMW would certainly have lost the 1900 strike. And quite possibly the decisive contest in 1902 would not have lasted five months or resulted in secure anthracite-region unionization.

The role of East European nationalities in the hard-coal fields suggests broader implications in the relationship between American unionism and immigration. The experience in the anthracite area indicates that early labor leaders really knew little about the needs of the unskilled foreign-born workers. Although migrants generally arrived not as individuals but as part of a group, and aimed by mutual self-help to reestablish their culture, the golden opportunity that communal organization offered to labor was ignored. The reconstructed settlements of Slavs in America were the adjustment mechanism to acclimate each newcomer into the new environment; if early organizers had selected, guided, and directed community leaders as John Fahy did, the immigrant social units, already sensitive to industrial injustice, would have "educated" the later greenhorns in due course. Except for the language barrier, the task for union officials would not have been difficult, for immigrants showed repeatedly that with grievances, regardless of a union's presence, they could strike and strike hard. Other disputes besides Lattimer—the Chicago stockyards unrest from 1900 to 1904, the conflicts in steel as mentioned, and the Lawrence and Paterson textile outbreaks in 1912 and 1913—all tell of Slavs in the "front rank."[9]

Even immigration historians have yet to describe in detail the vitality of the neighborhood in the life of the Slavic rank and file. This study, although it has not indicated exactly what particular force inside these colonies possessed leadership, asserts the militant potential of an immigrant community in labor affairs. Such an analysis must weaken the generalization of the Slav in America as thoroughly conservative and tradition oriented. In a strike, change was his goal, and his methods were radical; at these times the "simple peasant" forgot the

213

status-quo nature of his past. The assertions that the pre-World-War-I effort of labor organizers failed because it could not break down the stubborn conservatism of the immigrants are invalid. Certainly individuals such as mine superintendent Gomer Jones, policeman George Kellner, and even President John Mitchell, would not endorse such a view.

Rather than an immigrant responsibility for union failure, the greater weakness rests with labor itself. On occasion unusually perceptive observers of the time begged those, labor leaders in particular, who dealt closely with the East European American to adapt their organizational techniques to sociological realities. An astute critic, Dr. Peter Roberts, referred to the East European workman as "ready clay in the hands of the molders of industrial relationships . . . a tremendous asset . . . or a great peril *according to the way he is handled and led.*"[10] The United Mine Workers certainly heeded that advice. Another contemporary expert on labor relations warned union officials that their job of recruitment required flexibility; labor should educate workers of all kinds, whatever their sex or *nationality*:

> It is because many trade unions have so largely failed in organizing unskilled and women workers, and have been unable to cope with the problem of maintaining stable organizations among American wage earners of these classes that they have also failed to organize or hold immigrant men and women in their ranks. After such failures it is easy to blame the "foreigners" if they happen to be the people involved.[11]

214

Other authors pointed out that recent immigrants might have weakened unions simply by their newness, rather than because of any racial trait; and still others concluded that ethnic origin was probably neither a bar nor a stimulus to unionization.

If the early unionists had accepted the former peasant as he first settled in America and gauged their organizing efforts to his cultural makeup, they would have gained a mighty force in their struggle with management as John Fahy and Ben James discovered. An economist and labor official has concluded recently that today unions have learned a lesson: "There are no insuperable ethnic barriers to union organization if the union wants to organize."[12]

Finally the subject himself may have spoken to posterity. Just before the critical 1902 contest the *United Mine Workers' Journal* on April 17 published a letter allegedly from an average Slavic mineworker. Whether or not authentic, it does explain in his own style the enigma of the moment: the "Hungarian," his sentiments, his work mobility, his providence, and his belligerence in labor's "front rank."

Vell, everybody says, "Now vat is gonta do—strike?" Yes. No. Vich everybody talk for dot business. I see now same like before, troubles. Vach it. I know I see lots of peoples fixing cellar for coal, same for store and butcher. Vell, dot's all right. Lotsa eat, no work, dot's good. Vat's a matter fer you. Look in Vilkesbarre dot Hungarian fellows make de strike and Sheriff Martin right away fixin. Dots no business for de free country. All de same for

215

I don't care dots never work. I got it house, I leaven women stay. Dots me right away go for Pittsburg. Dot me strong man. I don't afraid for lots a fellows. I vas for old country soldier. Old country soldier no same like dis country. Old country everybody must go for soldier, dis country you no like soldier, no must go. Dot's all right, vy sure. Vell dots me must go home. I livin in Springfield sometime you come for my house. I fixing for lots a good time. Vell good bye.

Yours truly
Joe Knowitallski

Notes

INTRODUCTION

1. I will use the terms "East European" and "Slav" interchangeably, although ethnically this is incorrect. Lithuanians and other nationalities of the area are not Slavic. I use the terms of contemporary social observers to avoid confusion.

CHAPTER I: THE LOCALE

1. The family crest of a crowned bear holding a club was a fitting one. See Robert J. Spence, *John Markle, Representative American* (New York, 1929).
2. The saboteurs were chiefly the Pennsylvania and Lehigh Valley roads. See Eliot Jones, *Anthracite Coal Combination in the United States with Some Account of the Early Development of the Anthracite Industry* (Cambridge, Mass., 1914), pp. 40, 44–46; Arthur E. Suf-

fern, *Conciliation and Arbitration in the Coal Industry of America* (Boston, 1915), p. 223.

CHAPTER II: FROM OLD WORLD TO NEW

1. The most complete collection in English is of course in famous William I. Thomas and Florian Znaniecki, *The Polish Peasant in Europe and America* (5 vols., Boston, 1918-1920), from which I have drawn freely; and in Polish, *Pamietniki Emigrantów* (Warsaw, 1961), unfortunately containing only recent correspondence.

2. Tables that illustrate the shift are in Henry Pratt Fairchild, *Immigration* (New York, 1928), p. 135, and *Annual Report of the Commissioner General of Immigration for the Year Ended June 30, 1904* (Washington, D. C., 1904), pp. 31–35. Hereafter these reports will be designated by year. The 1860 figures for Germany probably indicated German-speaking territories outside Austria-Hungary.

3. See Frank Julian Warne, *The Immigrant Invasion* (New York, 1913), facing p. 64. The author had been an official of the 1910 census.

4. Before 1899, immigration data referred to "country of origin," and since neither Poland nor Lithuania was independent, the figures are imprecise. "Poland" probably refers to Congress Poland under Russian rule, and such figures would include Lithuanians, Jews, Russians, and others. Investigators find difficulty in distinguishing early Lithuanian newcomers. Unfortunately they did not feel any national consciousness before about 1880 and called themselves Poles or, at times, Russians. Therefore this study will restrict its comments about that time to the Poles, with the assumption that this will include most of the Lithuanians.

5. J. Grabiec, *Wspołczesna Polska w Cyfrach i Factach* (Cracow, 1912), p. 131; Felix Thomas Seroczynski,

"Poles in the United States," in *The Catholic Encyclopedia,* Vol. XII (1911), p. 205.

6. From American census data in Emily Greene Balch, *Our Slavic Fellow-Citizens* (New York, 1910), p. 132.
7. My own estimate from Joseph S. Roucek, "Poles in the United States," *Baltic and Scandanavian Countries,* Vol. III (January, 1937), p. 6; X. Waclaw Kruszka, *Historja Polska w Ameryce* (Milwaukee, 1937), Vol. I, p. 584; Erasme Piltz, *Petite Encyclopédie Polonaise* (Paris, 1916), p. 282; and H. H. Fisher, *America and the New Poland* (New York, 1928), p. 55. Authorities disagree radically about these figures in some cases, and one must make rather difficult reconciliations. Nevertheless there is some consensus on the proportions, which are therefore probably more accurate than the absolute figures.
8. See Seroczynski, "Poles in the United States," p. 205; and U. S. Senate, 61st Congress, 3rd Session, *Reports of the Immigration Commission: Emigration Conditions in Europe* (Washington, D. C., 1911), p. 30.
9. I include farm laborers, since the immigrants may not have understood whether to give their old or intended occupation.
10. Professor George Pierson of Yale University made this observation of nationality pioneers a "law of migrability." From a paper given at a meeting of the Organization of American Historians, April 23, 1965, in Kansas City, Mo.
11. A decrease of 18.3 percent in the number of landed Polish peasants occurred from 1824 to 1880. Francis Bujak, *Poland's Economic Development* (London, 1926), p. 39.
12. *Ibid.*
13. U. S. Department of State, *Reports of the Consular Offi-*

cers of the United States (Washington, D. C., 1887), p. 164.

14. See Irena Spustek, *Polacy w Petrogrodzie* (Warsaw, 1966), p. 26.

15. This static environment, related in Oscar Handlin, *The Uprooted* (New York, 1951), Chapter I, and specified in Thomas and Znaniecki, *The Polish Peasant,* Vol. I passim, is possibly overdrawn. The Old World primary community had already broken down somewhat before migration to America as a result of European industrialization. See the suggestions of Frank Thistlethwaite, "Migration from Europe Overseas in the Nineteenth and Twentieth Centuries," in Herbert Moller, ed., *Population Movements in Modern European History* (New York, 1964), pp. 73–92.

16. Poland, Chief Bureau of Statistics, *Concise Statistical Yearbook of Poland, 1937* (Warsaw, 1937), pp. 40, 43; Polish National Committee of America, *Polish Encyclopedia* (3 vols., Geneva, 1924), Vol. II, p. 773.

17. Bujak, *Poland's Economic Development,* p. 49; Jerzy Zubrzycki, *Polish Immigrants in Britain* (The Hague, 1956), p. 13.

18. Poland, *Catalogue of the Polish Pavilion at the World's Fair* (New York, 1939), A72; Zubrzycki, *Polish Immigrants in Britain,* p. 11; see also William J. Rose, *Poland: Old and New* (London, 1948), p. 23.

19. Geoffrey Drage, *Russian Affairs* (London, 1904), p. 323.

20. In the famous peasant epic, *The Peasants,* the community pitied the landless: "A man without land is like a man without legs: he crawls about and cannot get anywhere." Ladislas Reymont, *The Peasants* (New York, 1925), Vol. II, p. 77. And another quotation: "Such is the nature of a peasant that even if it should mean untimely digging his own grave, he would still

strive to buy a piece of this holy earth." Quoted in Elsa Bernault, "Polish Peasant Autobiographies" (Unpublished Ph.D. dissertation, Columbia University, 1950), p. 81.

21. Henry K. Frankel, *Poland: The Struggle for Power* (London, 1946), p. 58.

22. Calculated from Piltz, *Petite Encyclopédie Polonaise,* p. 364; Edgar Sydenstricker, "Collective Bargaining in the Anthracite Coal Industry," *Bulletin of the United States Bureau of Labor Statistics,* No. 191 (March, 1916), p. 16; Edward Young, *Special Report on Immigration* (Washington, D.C., 1872), Vol. IX; Balch, *Our Slavic Fellow-Citizens,* p. 56; Edith Abbot, "The Wages of Unskilled Labor in the United States," *Journal of Political Economy,* Vol. XIII (June, 1905), p. 365; House of Representatives, 58th Congress, 2nd Session, Document No. 732, U. S. Department of Commerce and Labor, Bureau of Statistics, *Special Consular Reports: Emigration to the United States* (Washington, D.C., 1904), p. 48. The Stettin Consul, John Kehl, said that American employers paid three times as much as Germans. *Ibid.,* p. 69.

23. Jeremiah W. Jenks and W. Jett Lauck, *The Immigration Problem* (New York, 1926), p. 20.

24. Balch described the persuaders as doing "little more than greasing the wheels" for Slavic immigration. Balch, *Our Slavic Fellow-Citizens,* p. 53.

25. The famous Polish writer Sienkiewicz wrote a short novel with the title *For Bread* and used the expression to denote the post-1870 mass emigration. Some proof of similar Slovak motivation is a translation entitled *Za Chłebom Do Ameriky* (To America for Bread) (Elmhurst, N.Y., n.d.).

26. Richmond Mayo-Smith, *Emigration and Immigration* (New York, 1908), pp. 30–33; *Immigration Commis-*

sion: Emigration Conditions, p. 53; Fisher, *America and the New Poland,* p. 54; Jadwiga Karlowiczowa, *Historya Zwiazku Polek w Ameryce* (Chicago, 1938), p. 1; Walter F. Willcox, ed., *International Migration* (2 vols., New York, 1929), Vol. II, p. 536; Fox, *Poles in America* (New York, 1922), p. 42; Thomas and Znaniecki, *Polish Peasant,* Vol. V, p. 6; Karol Wachtl, *Polonja w Ameryce* (Philadelphia, 1944), p. 25.

27. "The peasant eager for land, attached passionately to the earth, makes all possible sacrifices for it. He goes to find money in America in the crushing labor of the mines and factories." Posner, "Les Forces Sociales de la Pologne," p. 238.

28. Balch, *Our Slavic Fellow-Citizens,* p. 49.

29. Thomas and Znaniecki, *Polish Peasant,* Vol. I, p. 192.

30. See the political manipulations of the North German Lloyd and Hamburg-American Lines in local Polish government in the report of Consul Rawicz, Warsaw, in U.S. Department of State, *Reports of Diplomatic and Consular Officers concerning Emigration from Europe to the United States* (Washington, D.C., 1889), p. 145, and Edward A. Steiner, *On the Trail of the Immigrant* (New York, 1906), p. 31.

31. European evidence is in *Immigration Commission: Emigration Conditions* (Washington, D.C., 1911), pp. 96–97; Report of Consul Diederich, Bremen, *Special Consular Reports: Emigration to the United States,* pp. 47, 53; House of Representatives, 50th Congress, 1st Session, Miscellaneous Document No. 572, *Testimony Taken by the Select Committee of the House of Representatives to Inquire into the Alleged Violation of the Laws Prohibiting the Importation of Contract Laborers, Paupers, Convicts, and Other Causes* (Washington, D.C., 1888), p. 36. American percentages can be calculated from *Immigration Commission: Emigration Conditions,*

p. 71; Howard B. Grose, *Aliens or Americans?* (New York, 1906), p. 77; House of Representatives, 57th Congress, 1st Session, Document No. 184, *Reports of the Industrial Commission, Reports on Immigration, Including Testimony, With Review and Digest and Special Reports* (Washington, D.C., 1901), Vol. XV, pp. xviii, 11; and Charlotte Erickson, *American Industry and the European Immigrant 1860–1885* (Cambridge, Mass., 1957), p. 195.

32. Steiner, *On the Trail of the Immigrant,* p. 198.
33. Entry Books of St. Joseph's Home, 1897–1903; Frank J. Sheridan, "Italian, Slavic, and Hungarian Unskilled Laborers in the United States," *Bulletin of the Bureau of Labor,* No. 72 (September, 1907), p. 424; Thomas F. Meehan, "Emigrant Aid Societies," in Charles G. Herberman *et al.,* eds., *The Catholic Encyclopedia* (New York, 1909), Vol. V, p. 403.

CHAPTER III:
THE NATURE OF SLAVIC ANTHRACITE

1. V. Bartuśka, *Les Lituaniens d'Amerique* (Lausanne, 1918), p. 9.
2. Frank Julian Warne, *The Slav Invasion and the Mine Workers* (Philadelphia, 1904), pp. 51, 58–59; and Warne, "The Effect of Unionism upon the Mine Workers," *The Annals of the American Academy of Political and Social Science,* Vol. XXI (January, 1903), p. 29n.
3. *Annual Report of the Secretary of Internal Affairs of the Commonwealth of Pennsylvania,* Part III, *Industrial Statistics, 1903* (Harrisburg, 1904), Vol. XXXI, pp. 431–32. The relative positions were 31 and 16 percent, although some of the second generation Poles would bring the figures closer. The Irish were third with 8 percent.
4. The evidence for discernible East European communi-

ties is presented in many notes that follow in the form of histories of various Roman and Greek Catholic parishes. These brief accounts of individual neighborhoods, the author believes, are particularly good records of nationality development. Usually written for the congregation in the language of the nationality in observance of a church's anniversary, they tend to avoid the self-conscious ethnocentrism common in general group biographies written in English. Most of the writers were parish members themselves who faithfully recorded the remembrances of older parishioners. And almost all refer to the multigroup origins and development of their neighborhoods. The best Polish parish chronology of the region is in X. Wacław Kruszka, *Historja Polska w Ameryce* (13 vols., Milwaukee, 1905–1908), Vol. XII, pp. 58–74, 83–116, 119–23.

5. *Ibid.,* p. 60; Rev. Stephen Makar, "Ukrainian Colonies in the United States," *Svoboda* (Mt. Carmel, Pa.), November 4, 1897, p. 2.

6. *Evening Herald* (Shenandoah, Pa.), August 21, 1950, p. 4C.

7. Makar, "Ukrainian Colonies," November 25, 1897, p. 1, expresses his group's gratitude.

8. Jonas Zilius, *Lietuviai Amerikoj* (Plymouth, Pa., 1899), p. 33; Julian Bachinsky, *Ukrainian Immigration to the United States* (in Ukrainian) (Lwów, 1914), Vol. I, p. 286. Slavic "people traded with him, went to him with all their problems, and solicited his advice. His business was multifarious." Wasyl Halich, *Ukrainians in the United States* (Chicago, 1937), pp. 28–29.

9. Even in this ethnic conflict many Lithuanians remained loyal to Poles. Rev. Joseph A. Karalius, *Lietuviu Kataliku Sv. Jurgio 50 Metu Sukakciai Pamineti Leidinys, 1891–1941* (Shenandoah, Pa., 1941), pp. 10, 12, 30; for the dual nationality complexion of St. Stanislaus see

Złoty Jubileusz Parafii Sw. Stanislaus B. i M. w Shenan-doah, Pennsylvania (Shenandoah, 1948), p. 13.

10. Zilius, *Lietuviai Amerikoj,* p. 27; Kruszka, *Historja,* XII, pp. 64–67.

11. *Historia Polskich Parafij w Archidiecezii Filadelfijskiej* (Philadelphia, 1940), p. 90.

12. Zilius, *Lietuviai Amerikoj,* p. 64.

13. *Ibid.,* p. 69.

14. *Souvenir of the Golden Jubilee of Most Sacred Heart of Jesus and Mary Parish (1885–1935)* (Scranton, Pa., 1935), pp. 13, 15; *Golden Jubilee, 1904–1954, St. Mary's Mocanaqua, Pennsylvania* (Mocanaqua, Pa., 1954), p. 10; Zilius, *Lietuviai Amerikoj,* p. 75.

15. Zilius, *Lietuviai Amerikoj,* p. 58; *St. Casimir's Parish, Diamond Jubilee, 1881–1961* (Freeland, Pa., 1961), p. 21.

16. *Silver Jubilee of St. Stanislaus Parish, Summit Hill, Pa., May 1, 1949* (Summit Hill, Pa., 1949), p. 12; Joseph Zerbey, *History of Pottsville, Schuylkill County, Penn-sylvania* (5 vols., Pottsville, Pa., 1934–1935), Vol. IV, p. 1519; *Historia Polskich Parafij w Archidiecezji Fila-delfijskiej,* p. 97; Kruszka, *Historja,* XII, p. 109.

17. From the above survey it would be difficult to accept the assertion of A. Kaupas, "Lithuanians in America," *Charities and the Commons,* Vol. XIII (December 3, 1904), p. 233, that for the past ten years his group had "nothing in common" with Poles. He stated himself that the two had once been unified on the most intimate terms in Europe and America, built churches in common, and joined the same benevolent societies. Cf. Stanisław Osada, *Historya Zwiazku Narodowego Polskiego* (Chicago, 1905), pp. 519–22; Kruszka, *Historja,* XII, pp. 69–70.

18. The pattern is in Szawleski, *Wychodztwo Polskie w Stanach Zjednoczonych Ameryki* (Warsaw, 1924), pp.

225

25–26, for the Poles; Zilius, *Lietuviai Amerikoj,* passim for Lithuanians; James Zatko, "The Social History of Slovak Immigrants in America" (Unpublished M.A. thesis, University of Notre Dame, 1954), pp. 25–26, 37, 40–41; and Bachinsky, *Ukrainian Immigration,* pp. 185–93.

19. Report of a newspaperman viewing the arrival of an immigrant train at Wilkes-Barre, 1884. *Wilkes-Barre Union Leader,* January 28, 1884, p. 1.

20. Accommodations of Mrs. Haley, Thomas Grady, and Patrick Donahue, Mahanoy City, 1882, in *Weekly Miners' Journal* (Pottsville, Pa.), July 28, 1882, p. 6.

21. Of course there is no one figure for the number of boarders per shanty. Houses were of different sizes, and American authorities undoubtedly emphasized the exceptions. One heard of forty in a house; another, fourteen in a room; and a third, twenty-one in a shack.

22. See Edward Alsworth Ross, "The Slav in America," *The Century Illustrated Magazine,* Vol. LXXXVIII (August, 1914), pp. 592, 594.

23. Peter Roberts, *Anthracite Coal Communities* (New York, 1904), p. 106.

24. Before about 1886 miners received coal free. After that date the operators charged employees about $1.50 per month. But often the Slavs merely raided culm piles. In any event they got fuel cheaper than did the public at large. Henry George, "Labor in Pennsylvania," *North American Review,* Vol. CCCLVII (August, 1886), p. 175; Peter Roberts, *Anthracite Coal Industry* (New York, 1901), p. 133; Frank Julian Warne, "The Real Cause of the Miners' Strike," *The Outlook,* Vol. LXXI (August 30, 1902), p. 1055.

25. I am assuming that the boardinghouse landlord received all the rent and most of the board, for the immigrant may have had to pay for part of the food himself.

Sources in the 1880's stated that rent for these quarters was between one and two dollars a month, and the total living cost for single Poles was about nine dollars. "Not a Dangerous Class," *New York Times,* February 18, 1884, p. 2; *The Philadelphia Record,* August 4, 1888, p. 3; House of Representatives, 50th Congress, 1st Session, Miscellaneous Document No. 572, *Testimony Taken by the Select Committee of the House of Representatives to Inquire into the Alleged Violation of Laws Prohibiting the Importation of Contract Laborers, Paupers, Convicts, and Other Causes* (Washington, D.C., 1888), p. 204.

26. William I. Thomas and Florian Znaniecki, *The Polish Peasant In Europe and America* (5 vols., Boston, 1918–1920), Vol. IV, p. 136. For a typical example see Edward Falkowski, "Polonia to America," *Common Ground,* Vol. II (Autumn, 1941), p. 29.

27. Roberts, *Communities,* pp. 52–53, 222–24, 242; Rev. Peter Roberts, "The Slavs in Anthracite Communities," *Charities and the Commons,* Vol. XIII (December 3, 1904), p. 219. One nationality historian had an interesting reason for the Pole's thirst for alcohol: the dust of the mine and factory. Leopold Caro, *Emigracya i Polityka Emigracyjna* (Poznan, 1914), p. 154.

28. The days after holidays or pay days, however, were not always normal. Employers complained that Slavs sometimes took additional time off to recuperate after particularly enthusiastic celebrations. *Reports of the Industrial Commission, Report on the Relations and Conditions of Capital and Labor Employed in the Mining Industry, Including Testimony, Review of Evidence, and Topical Digest* (Washington, D.C., 1901), Vol. XII, p. 671.

29. Owen R. Lovejoy, "Child Labor in the Coal Mines," *The Annals of the American Academy of Political and*

Social Science, Vol. XXVII (March, 1906), p. 40. The evil was not solely an East European practice but was probably more universal among them. Roberts, *Communities,* p. 176.

30. This does not exhaust the occupations of East Europeans, for employers also hired them for general maintenance labor, timbermen, fan turners, and other unskilled work. Each job progression, of course, paid more. The "miner" was in reality a semiskilled worker responsible for the actual mining process, securing safety measures, handling the charge, pulling down the coal, and supervising his "helper," the Slav.

31. None of these was more than 6 percent Polish. The largest number was 24 of 421 firemen. Report of the W. B. Meredith Committee in *The Legislative Record for the Session, 1897* (Harrisburg, 1897), Vol. II, p. 2675.

32. Old slate pickers got slightly more. *Annual Report of the Secretary of Internal affairs for the Commonwealth of Pennsylvania for 1874–1875,* Part III, *Industrial Statistics,* Vol. III (Harrisburg, 1876), pp. 487–92; *Annual Report of the Secretary of Internal Affairs for the Commonwealth of Pennsylvania for 1875–1876,* Part III, *Industrial Statistics,* Vol. III (Harrisburg, 1877), pp. 362, 401, 462.

33. Estimated from Edward Parker, "Coal," in U.S. Department of the Interior, U.S. Geological Survey, *Mineral Resources of the United States: 1912,* Part II, *Non-Metals* (Washington, D.C., 1913), p. 673; and *Report of the Industrial Commission on Transportation* (Washington, D.C., 1901), Vol. IX, p. 574.

34. *Reports of the Industrial Commission, . . . Conditions . . . in the Mining Industry. . . . ,* Vol. XII, pp. 160–64.

35. Emily Greene Balch, "Our Slavic Fellow-Citizens: Women and the Household," *Charities and the Commons,* Vol. XIX (October 5, 1907), p. 781.

36. Author's italics. H. H. Spayd, "The Early Settlement of Minersville and History of Its Schools," *Publications of the Historical Society of Schuylkill County,* Vol. I (Pottsville, 1907), p. 76.

37. Peter Paul Jonitis, "Acculturation of the Lithuanians of Chester, Pennsylvania" (Unpublished Ph.D. dissertation, University of Pennsylvania, 1951), p. 274.

38. House of Representatives, 57th Congress, 1st Session, Document No. 184, *Reports of the Industrial Commission, Reports on Immigration, Including Testimony, With Review and Digests and Special Reports* (Washington, D.C., 1901), Vol. XV, p. 44; *The Philadelphia Record,* July 31, 1888, p. 1; Roberts, *Communities,* p. 116. Probably only the depression of the mid-1890's belied these figures.

39. Caro, *Emigracya i Polityka Emigracyjna,* p. 154, felt that Poles retained about fourteen of thirty-three dollars monthly; *The Reading Eagle,* January 8, 1888, p. 1, estimated that they accumulated five hundred dollars in a "few years"; and Warne, *The Slav Invasion,* p. 67, as much as two-thirds of the bachelors' income.

40. Rowland Tappan Berthoff, *British Immigrants in Industrial America* (Cambridge, Mass., 1953), p. 126.

41. *Annual Report of the Secretary of Internal Affairs for the Commonwealth of Pennsylvania for 1882–1883,* Part III, *Industrial Statistics,* Vol. XI (Harrisburg, 1884), p. 67; New York, *Third Annual Report of the Bureau of Statistics of Labor for the Year 1885* (Albany, 1886), p. 511; Zilius, *Lietuviai Amerikoj,* p. 41; *New York Evening Post,* October 6, 1900, in the (Mrs. John) *Markle Scrapbooks* in the Hazleton Public Library, hereafter MS; Kenneth D. Miller, *The Czecho-Slovaks in America* (New York, 1922), p. 63; Peter P. Yurchak, *The Slovaks: Their History and Traditions* (Whiting, Indiana, 1946), p. 181.

229

42. "Not a Dangerous Class," p. 2.
43. *The Philadelphia Record,* July 31, 1888, p. 1.
44. Roberts, *Communities,* p. 253.
45. Charles W. Coulter, *The Poles in Cleveland* (Cleveland, 1919), p. 11.
46. Roberts, *Communities,* pp. 41–43.

CHAPTER IV: EARLY UNION FAILURES

1. Elsie Glück, *John Mitchell, Miner* (New York, 1929), p. 68.
2. Henry Rood, "A Pennsylvania Colliery Village: A Polyglot Community," *The Century Illustrated Monthly Magazine,* Vol. LV (April, 1898), p. 809; Rood, "The Public and the Coal Conflict," *The North American Review,* Vol. CLXXI (October, 1905), p. 605.
3. Edward Alsworth Ross, "The Old World in the New: Economic Consequences," *The Century Illustrated Monthly Magazine,* Vol. LXV (November, 1913), p. 30.
4. Alan Conway, ed., *The Welsh in America: Letters from Immigrants* (Minneapolis, 1961), p. 166.
5. Clifton Yearley, *Enterprise and Anthracite: Economics and Democracy in Schuylkill County, 1820–1875* (Baltimore, 1961), pp. 177–78, 182; Edgar Sydenstricker, "Collective Bargaining in the Anthracite Industry," *Bulletin of the United States Bureau of Labor Statistics,* No. 191 (March, 1916), p. 13; A. J. McCafferty, *Locust Gap, Northumberland County, Pennsylvania: A History* (n.p., 1929), p. 26, in offices of the *Daily Item* (Mt. Carmel, Pa.); Peter Roberts, *Anthracite Coal Industry* (New York, 1901), p. 172; House of Representatives, 57th Congress, 1st Session, Document No. 184, *Reports of the Industrial Commission, Reports on Immigration, Including Testimony, With Review and Digest and Special Reports* (Washington, D.C., 1901), Vol. XV, p. 405.

6. Yearley, *Enterprise and Anthracite,* pp. 184–85.
7. Charles Edward Killeen, "John Siney. The Pioneer in American Industrial Government" (Unpublished Ph.D. dissertation, University of Wisconsin, 1942), p. 142; Roberts, *Anthracite Coal Industry,* p. 176; Joseph D. Weeks, *Industrial Conciliation and Arbitration in New York, Ohio, and Pennsylvania* (Boston, 1881), p. 22.
8. George O. Virtue, "The Anthracite Mine Laborers," *Bulletin of the Bureau of Labor No. 13* (November, 1897), pp. 744; John Maguire, "Early Pennsylvania Coal Mine Legislation," *Publications of the Historical Society of Schuylkill County,* Vol. IV (Pottsville, 1914), p. 338, memoirs of a WBA leader.
9. The best brief account of events in the period is in Marvin Schlegel, "The Workingmen's Benevolent Association," *Pennsylvania History,* Vol. X (October, 1943), pp. 243 ff.
10. Yearley, *Enterprise and Anthracite,* pp. 186–87, and Wayne G. Broehl, *The Molly Maguires* (Cambridge, Mass., 1964), pp. 109–11.
11. The distinction between appearance and reality is in Yearley, *Enterprise and Anthracite,* p. 187.
12. The north-south antagonisms are in Welsh letters, in Conway, *The Welsh in America,* p. 193, further supported by Broehl, *The Molly Maguires,* pp. 97, 98, 101, 112, 185; Roberts, *Anthracite Coal Industry,* p. 176; Andrew Roy, *A History of the Coal Miners of the United States* (Columbus, Ohio, 1903), p. 89.
13. Marvin Schlegel, *Ruler of the Reading* (Harrisburg, 1947), p. 22.
14. *Weekly Miners' Journal* (Pottsville), January 15, 1875, p. 42; April 2, 1875, pp. 226, 228.
15. *Ibid.,* January 15, 1875, p. 50; March 5, 1875, p. 162; April 23, 1875, supplement; *New York Times,* March 6, 1875, p. 3. The reader will note extensive use here-

after of New York and Philadelphia papers for 1875 and 1877. The author felt that their correspondents' reports were particularly sensitive. Even when the local press criticised the larger journals for sensationalism, it still republished often the accounts of the latter. See especially the *Weekly Miners' Journal* below in 1877.

16. *Weekly Miners' Journal,* April 2, 1875, p. 228.
17. *New York Times,* March 6, 1875, p. 3.
18. *The Times* (Philadelphia), June 3, 1875, p. 1.
19. From *Summit Hill Intelligencer* in *Weekly Miners' Journal,* June 4, 1875, supplement. Another, similar letter, although more critical of union leadership, is in *ibid.,* May 21, 1875, supplement. Welsh's disappointment is in *ibid.,* April 9, 1875, p. 228; April 23, 1875, supplement.
20. *New York Times,* March 6, 1875, p. 3; March 24, 1875, p. 1.
21. Published in *ibid.,* June 18, 1875, p. 389.
22. Joseph F. Patterson, "Old W.B.A. Days," *Publications of the Historical Society of Schuylkill County,* Vol. II (Pottsville, 1910), p. 366. The author was an early WBA official.
23. The present standard on the society is Broehl, *Molly Maguires.* The spectacle of the many killings, especially the near hysteria in mid-1875, the trials, and mass hangings, has provided a legend which old-timers love to relate. However the author believes the incident has little real historical significance. See Yearley, *Enterprise and Anthracite,* p. 186. The memory of the Mollies was of far greater influence, possibly anesthetising Irish labor radicalism in later disputes. Of course, evidence for such an assertion is unavailable, but see Broehl, *Molly Maguires,* p. 350.
24. *New York Times,* April 8, 1875, p. 7; April 9, 1875, p. 7.

25. *Public Ledger,* May 11, 1875, p. 1; *Philadelphia Times,* May 12, 1875, p. 1. For other bituminous scabs see *New York Times,* May 4, 1875, p. 7.
26. Very few Slavs, if any, lived in the middle field in 1875. *The Philadelphia Record,* July 31, 1888, p. 1; Kruszka, *Historja,* XII, p. 109.
27. *Weekly Miners' Journal,* September 14, 1877, p. 6. See also descriptions of conditions in Pennsylvania, *General Assembly, Report of the Committee to Investigate the Rail Road Riots in July, 1877* (Harrisburg, 1878), pp. 4, 727–728, 776; hereafter Pennsylvania, *Riots.*
28. *New York Herald,* May 20, 1877, p. 9. Also see New *York Sun,* August 4, 1877, p. 3.
29. *Annual Report of the Secretary of Internal Affairs of the Commonwealth of Pennsylvania for 1875–1876* (Harrisburg, 1877), p. 816. The best contemporary account is the testimony in Pennsylvania, *Riots.*
30. The mayor's account appears factually accurate. Pennsylvania, *Riots,* pp. 28–29, 706–709, 715.
31. *Weekly Miners' Journal,* August 3, 1877, p. 1; August 24, p. 3; *New York Herald,* July 28, 1877, p. 5; August 2, p. 4; August 3, p. 4; August 4, p. 2. Some Lehigh workers were out of work not because of a strike but rather for the lack of railroad cars. *Evening Herald* (Shenandoah, Pa.), July 30, 1877, p. 1; August 1, p. 1.
32. Terence V. Powderly, *Thirty Years of Labor, 1859 to 1889* (Columbus, Ohio, 1890), p. 209; George E. Stevenson, *Reflections of An Anthracite Engineer* (New York, 1931), p. 183; *Weekly Miners' Journal,* August 10, 1877, p. 1. The popular hysteria associating any union with the "Molly" conspiracy probably killed any organizational project. *Journal of the Senate of the Commonwealth of Pennsylvania, for the Adjourned Session Begun at Harrisburg on the First Day of January, 1878* (Harrisburg, 1878), p. 1059; Samuel C. Logan, *A*

City's Danger and Defense (Scranton, 1887), pp. 200, 206; *New York Herald,* August 4, 1877, p. 2; Pennsylvania, *Riots,* pp. 30, 46, 774.

33. *Weekly Miners' Journal,* August 3, 1877, p. 7; October 5, p. 2.

34. *Ibid.,* August 31, 1877, p. 6; September 14, p. 6; *New York Times,* October 18, 1877, p. 1.

35. His "Germans" were "artisans and skilled workmen," so probably not Slavs. Logan, *A City's Danger,* p. 57. Pennsylvania, *Riots,* p. 728.

36. Thomas Murphy, *History of Lackawanna County, Pennsylvania* (Topeka, Kansas, 1928), Vol. I, p. 384.

37. *Weekly Miners' Journal,* August 10, 1877, p. 3.

38. Julian Bachinsky, *Ukrainian Immigration to the United States* (in Ukrainian), (Lwów, 1914), Vol. I, p. 135.

39. Testimony of Jules Rosendale, House of Representatives, 57th Congress, 1st Session, Document No. 184, *Reports of the Industrial Commission on Immigration* (Washington, D. C., 1901), Vol. XV, p. 191.

CHAPTER V:
A SLAVIC COMMUNITY STRIKES

1. John R. Commons, in House of Representatives, 57th Congress, 1st Session, Document No. 184, *Reports of the Industrial Commission on Immigration* (Washington, D. C., 1901), Vol. XV, p. 405.

2. House of Representatives, 50th Congress, 1st Session, Miscellaneous Document No. 572, *Testimony Taken by the Select Committee of the House of Representatives to Inquire into the Alleged Violation of the Laws Prohibiting the Importation of Contract Laborers, Paupers, Convicts, and Other Causes* (Washington, D. C., 1888), p. 213. See also *The Philadelphia Record,* August 1, 1888, p. 1, in which an operator says that imports are part of a scheme to break down strikes.

3. John Graham Brooks, *The Social Unrest: Studies in Labor and Socialist Movements* (New York, 1909), p. 354.

4. Waldo E. Fisher, "Anthracite," in Labor Committee of the Twentieth Century Fund, *How Collective Bargaining Works* (New York, 1942), p. 285.

5. Robert J. Cornell, *The Anthracite Coal Strike of 1902* (Published Ph.D. dissertation, Catholic University of America, 1957), p. 31.

6. *The Evening Leader* (Wilkes-Barre), June 3, 1884, p. 1.

7. *The Evening Leader,* May 19, 1884, p. 1.

8. *Weekly Miners' Journal,* December 4, 1885, p. 3.

9. *Daily News-Dealer,* December 19, 1886, p. 9; and see August 6, p. 1, for other conflicts.

10. *Weekly Miners' Journal,* May 27, 1887, p. 3.

11. This was probably Joseph Janiski, head of the town's Polish Kosciuszko Guards. *History of Schuylkill County, Pennsylvania* (New York, 1881), p. 381; *Semi-Weekly Standard,* April 4, 1885, p. 3. A major and constant inaccuracy in newspapers is the spelling of Slavic names; they change almost with each citation.

12. *Daily News-Dealer,* April 4, 1886, p. 1; April 11, 1886, p. 1; July 24, 1886, p. 1; October 3, 1886, p. 1.

13. Letter to George W. Polandz, July 31, 1889, quoted in Sister William Marie Turnbach, R.S.M., "The Attitudes of Terence V. Powderly toward Minority Groups (1879–1893)" (Unpublished M.A. thesis, Catholic University of America, 1956), pp. 33–34, 51.

14. The reporter exaggerated, perhaps, but only slightly. *Weekly Miners' Journal,* October 28, 1887, p. 1.

15. *New York Herald,* April 8, 1888, p. 9. See also the Lehigh epitaph of despair in *The Evening Leader,* March 11, 1888, p. 6.

16. Quoted in the *New York Times,* January 1, 1888, p. 2.

17. Quoted in the *Reading Eagle,* January 2, 1888, p. 3.
18. *Evening Herald,* January 30, 1888, p. 1.
19. *Reading Eagle,* February 3, 1888, p. 1; *Evening Herald,* January 29, 1888, p. 1; February 2, p. 1.
20. *Evening Herald,* January 29, 1888, p. 1.
21. From the *Lansford Record* (Pennsylvania) in *ibid.*
22. *The Philadelphia Record,* February 5, 1888, p. 1.
23. *Ibid.,* August 1, 1888, p. 1. Italians are in the former figure.
24. *Evening Herald,* January 7, 1888, p. 1.
25. *Reading Eagle,* January 20, 1888, p. 1.
26. *New York Times,* August 10, 1887, p. 1.
27. *Ibid.*
28. *The Evening Leader,* August 10, 1887, p. 4.
29. Andrew Malinsky, Michael Yopiski, and Thomas Isaacs were held. *The Evening Leader,* August 25, 1887, p. 4.
30. "Italians" and "Hungarians" were really indistinguishable. *Ibid.,* September 14, 1887, p. 1. See the unyielding determination later among "Italians" in *The Wilkes-Barre Record,* December 14, 1887, p. 1.
31. *The Weekly Item* (Mt. Carmel, Pa.), January 21, 1888, p. 1.
32. *Third Annual Report of the State Board of Health and Vital Statistics of the Commonwealth of Pennsylvania* (Harrisburg, 1888), p. 76. An American warned of the effects of such poverty: he heard a concertina playing the "Marseillaise" among the shacks. *New York Herald,* January 31, 1888, p. 4.
33. *New York Herald,* February 5, 1888, p. 16; *Daily Republican* (Pottsville), February 2, 1888, p. 1; *The Reading Eagle,* February 2, 1888, p. 1; and the testimony in House of Representatives, 50th Congress, 2nd Session, Report No. 4147, *Labor Troubles in the Anthracite Regions* (Washington, D. C., 1889), pp. 145–46.
34. *The Reading Eagle,* February 2, 1888, p. 1; *The Wilkes-*

Barre Record, February 3, 1888, p. 2. *The Reading Eagle,* February 3, 1888, p. 1, says a similar incident occurred in the evening.

35. *Evening Herald,* February 4, 1888, p. 1.
36. *Ibid.*
37. *Ibid.*
38. *Daily Republican,* February 4, 1888, p. 1.
39. *Evening Herald,* February 4, 1888, p. 1.
40. *The Reading Eagle,* February 5, 1888, p. 1; *The Catholic* (Pittsburgh, Pa.), February 11, 1888, p. 5; *Evening Herald,* February 6, 1888, p. 1; *The Times* (Philadelphia), February 4, 1888, p. 1.
41. *Evening Herald,* February 6, 1888, p. 1.
42. *Weekly Miners' Journal,* February 10, 1888, p. 1.
43. *Daily Republican,* February 6, 1888, p. 1.
44. *The Reading Eagle,* February 4, 1888, p. 1.
45. *Ibid.,* February 5, 1888, p. 1.
46. Ordinarily the position of the Slavic clergy should have been a critical one with the prevalent belief of the priest's power over his parishioners. But the immigrant largely ignored his religious leader's interference in his job. Peter Roberts, *Anthracite Coal Communities* (New York, 1904), p. 36.
47. *Daily Republican,* February 7, 1888, p. 1.
48. *Public Ledger,* February 8, 1888, p. 1; *The Times* (Philadelphia), February 8, 1888, p. 1.
49. *New York Times,* February 5, 1888, p. 1.
50. *Daily Republican,* February 8, 1888, p. 1.
51. A virulent nativist, Olney Searles, "The Coal Strike," *North American Review,* Vol. CXLVI (March, 1888), p. 342.
52. *The Reading Eagle,* February 5, 1888, p. 1.
53. *Evening Leader,* September 13, 1888, p. 1.

CHAPTER VI:
AN INTERLUDE OF ATTEMPTED NOSTRUMS

1. *Daily News-Dealer,* September 4, 1889, p. 4.
2. *New York Herald,* September 30, 1900, in *Markle Scrapbooks,* Hazleton Public Library.
3. *John Swinton's Paper,* December, 1883, and January, 1884, passim.
4. House of Representatives, 57th Congress, 1st Session, Document No. 184, *Report of the Industrial Commission, Reports on Immigration, Including Testimony, With Review and Digests and Special Reports,* Vol. XV, pp. 417–19; Alexander Trachtenberg, *History of Legislation for the Protection of Coal Miners in Pennsylvania, 1824–1915* (New York, 1942), p. 135.
5. A former governor, William A. Stone, *The Tale of a Plain Man* (Philadelphia, 1918), p. 287.
6. The Senate vote was not available. The House vote was 144 to 5, with 55 abstentions. *The Legislative Record for the Session 1889,* Vol. II, April 22, 1889, pp. 1527–29, 1548.
7. *Wilkes-Barre Union Leader,* January 25, 1884, p. 1.
8. *Public Ledger,* April 9, 1890, p. 6. See also George O. Virtue, "The Anthracite Mine Laborers," *Bulletin of the Bureau of Labor,* No. 13 (November, 1897), pp. 752–53, and *Pottsville Republican,* September 20, 1897, p. 3.
9. *Wilkes-Barre Union Leader,* January 25, 1884, p. 1. Roberts felt that while they suffered at lower pay when they first arrived, "today" they are very assertive. In fact, "English-speaking employees will cut prices sooner than the Sclavs." Peter Roberts, *Anthracite Coal Communities* (New York, 1904), p. 39.
10. *Public Ledger,* April 9, 1890, p. 6.
11. *Reports of the Industrial Commission, Report on the Relations and Conditions of Capital and Labor Em-*

ployed in the Mining Industry, Including Testimony, Review of Evidence, and Topical Digest (Washington, D. C., 1901), Vol. XII, p. 655.

12. *Reports of the Inspector of Coal Mines of Pennsylvania, 1893* (Harrisburg, 1894), p. 7. Virtue, in "The Anthracite Mine Laborers," pp. 751–53, also stated that their accident frequency was not disproportionate.

13. His view was not anti-Slavic. *Report of the Bureau of Mines of the Department of Internal Affairs of Pennsylvania, 1901,* p. 249. One Polish miner told me that his experience was not unusual: in the late 1890's he bought his certificate for two shots of whiskey. Interview with Mr. Charles Kunkel, Springfield (Shamokin P.O.), Pennsylvania, May 1, 1962.

14. But for a six-weeks' strike the 1900 figure would have been higher and the 1901 number lower. Edward Parker, "Coal," in U.S. Department of the Interior, U.S. Geological Survey, *Mineral Resources of the United States: 1912,* Part II, *Non-Metals* (Washington, D. C., 1913), pp. 47, 49.

15. *Public Ledger,* March 29, 1890, p. 9.

16. Both are in *ibid*. The Shamokin area on the whole had less distress. Here, too, the Slav could easily get work. *Ibid.,* April 5, 1890, p. 6.

17. *The Press* (Philadelphia), April 8, 1894, p. 1.

18. *The Legislative Record for . . . 1897,* Vol. II, p. 2668.

19. Emily Greene Balch, "Our Slavic Fellow-Citizens: Slavs as Farmers," *Charities and the Commons,* Vol. XVIII (July 6, 1907), pp. 369, 372.

20. *United Mine Workers' Journal,* March 17, 1898, p. 1.

21. *The Freeland Press,* September 9, 1932, p. 1; "The Coal Strike: A Near-by View," *The Outlook,* Vol. LXXII (October 18, 1902) p. 402; interview with Joseph Anceravige, Mahanoy City, May 5, 1962, who knew Fahy.

22. *United Mine Workers' Journal,* December 20, 1894, p. 2.

23. *Ibid.,* February 7, 1895, p. 2.

24. Letter from Jim Dorset of Shamokin in *United Mine Workers' Journal,* July 18, 1895, p. 5. Fr. Jonas Zilius, *Lietuviai Amerikoj* (Plymouth, Pa., 1899), p. 29, testified to its initial success. It is entirely possible that in smaller hamlets such as these the foreign locals were actually Slavic rather than of one nationality or, if national in establishment, contained other foreigners later.

25. *United Mine Workers' Journal,* April 23, 1896, p. 5.

26. *Ibid.,* December 20, 1894, p. 2.

27. Fahy to Mitchell, August 2, 1899, *Mitchell Papers* in Archives, Catholic University, Washington, D. C., hereafter *MP.*

28. *The Weekly Item,* May 16, 1896, p. 3.

29. *United Mine Workers' Journal,* October 22, 1897, p. 1; November 5, p. 1; December 3, p. 1.

30. *Ibid.,* July 1, 1897, p. 1; August 12, p. 1.

CHAPTER VII: LEHIGH IN TURMOIL

1. His judgment. *Pottsville Republican,* September 11, 1897, p. 1.

2. *The Wilkes-Barre Record,* September 15, 1897, p. 2; *Wilkes-Barre Times,* August 27, 1897, p. 8.

3. *Wilkes-Barre Times,* August 17, 1897, p. 1.

4. *The Daily Standard,* August 17, 1897, p. 1.

5. The company did promise to look into Jones' behavior. *Pottsville Republican,* September 11, 1897, p. 1, asserted that privately the company admitted Jones' mistreatment of some mineworkers but refused to make it appear that it was knuckling under to employee dictation.

6. *Wilkes-Barre Times,* August 28, 1897, p. 1.

7. *Ibid.,* September 4, 1897, p. 1; *Evening Herald,* Septem-

ber 3, 1897, p. 1; September 4, 1897, p. 1. See also *The Mauch Chunk Democrat,* September 5, 1897, p. 4, on marchers' techniques.

8. *Wilkes-Barre Times,* September 6, 1897, p. 1; *The Daily Standard,* September 7, 1897; p. 1.

9. *The Daily Standard,* September 9, 1897, p. 1; September 10, p. 1.

10. The others are unknown. My estimate is from Zilius, *Lietuviai Amerikoj,* p. 60; Konstantin Čulen, "Lattimerska Jatka," *Jednota Kalendar* (1938), p. 50; Edward Pinkowski, *Lattimer Massacre* (Philadelphia, 1950), p. 15; *Tevyne,* Vol. II (October, 1897), p. 311.

11. *Pottsville Republican,* September 13, 1897, p 1.

12. As for some other groups the burial ceremonies have a special significance for the Slav and are disproportionately costly. See Helen Stankiewicz Zand, "Polish American Folkways," *Polish-American Studies,* Vol. XVII (July-December, 1960), pp. 100–104.

13. The court had reduced the number of defendants to sixty-eight. Henry W. Palmer, *Fifty Years at the Bar and in Politics* (Williamsport, Pa., 1913), p. 60. The author was a counsel for the defense. For the purpose of this study fixing the legal responsibility for the Lattimer episode is unnecessary. Despite protestations of a grossly unfair trial and cries of prejudice, the decision on the issue at hand was probably just. While Martin and his men deserved some punishment, the prosecution conducted its case poorly. For the activities of the prosecution and conclusion of the trial see *ibid.,* pp. 60–274; Pinkowski, *Lattimer Massacre,* pp. 27–40; *Pottsville Republican,* February 4, 7, 9, 10, 15–17, 25–26, 1898; March 2, 9; Čulen, "Lattimerska Jatka," pp. 55–61; and *Straż,* February 12, 1898, p. 1.

14. *Daily Miners' Journal,* September 18, 1897, p. 2; *The Wilkes-Barre Record,* September 18, 1897, p. 1.

15. *Wilkes-Barre Times,* September 17, 1897, p. 1.
16. *The Wilkes-Barre Record,* September 22, 1897, p. 1.
17. *The Sentinel,* September 7, 1897, in *United Mine Workers' Journal,* November 18, 1897, p. 1.
18. *Daily Miners' Journal,* September 14, 1897, in *United Mine Workers' Journal,* November 18, 1897, p. 2; *The Times* (Philadelphia), September 19, 1897, p. 5; *Daily Miners' Journal,* September 23, 1897, p. 1.
19. *Pottsville Republican,* September 14, 1897, p. 1.
20. Quoted in *United Mine Workers' Journal,* November 23, 1897, p. 2.

CHAPTER VIII: THE UMW's FIRST TEST

1. Paul de Rousiers, *Ranches, Farmes, et Usines* (Paris, 1899), p. 303.
2. His report is in *United Mine Workers' Journal,* March 31, 1898, p. 1.
3. In the fall of 1896 religious dissension broke out among certain Scranton Polish Catholics who disputed the Bishop's participation in local parish affairs. The issue basically centered over the inability of the Irish church hierarchy and a Polish congregation to reach agreement on certain aspects of control. The dissident group asked Reverend Francis Hodur, a Catholic priest at Nanticoke, to assist them. He did so and assumed leadership of this and, later, of other independence movements elsewhere which were united to form the Polish National Catholic Church. After attempts at mediation late in 1898 Rome excommunicated Hodur and his assistants. Among others, good accounts are Theodore Andrews, *Polish National Church in America and Poland* (London, 1953), and the official *Ksiega Pamiatkowa "33" w Trzydziestą Trzecią Rocznice Polsko Narodowego Katolickiego Kosciola w Ameryce* (Scranton, 1930).
4. *United Mine Workers' Journal,* April 21, 1898, p. 4.

5. His testimony in *Reports of the Industrial Commission, Report on the Relations and Conditions of Capital and Labor Employed in the Mining Industry, Including Testimony, Review of Evidence, and Topical Digest* (Washington, D. C., 1901), Vol. XII, p. 147.

6. *United Mine Workers' Journal,* August 24, 1899, p. 4; August 31, p. 1.

7. *Evening Leader,* September 2, 1899, p. 1.

8. *Ibid.,* August 1, 1899, p. 1; August 2, p. 1; August 8, p. 1; *United Mine Workers' Journal,* November 2, 1899, p. 1. The Susquehanna Coal Company Notebook at the Glen Lyon office says that the Nanticoke men quit on July 26 and the Glen Lyon men, August 5. A Mrs. Mary Waszkiewicz was the leading "amazon." *Evening Leader,* November 24, 1899, p. 1.

9. The outcome of the Pittston suspension is unknown. *Evening Leader,* September 2, 1899, p. 1; *United Mine Workers' Journal,* October 5, 1899, p. 1.

10. Fahy to Mitchell, November 14, 1899, in *John Mitchell Papers,* Catholic University Archives, Washington, D. C.

11. *United Mine Workers' Journal,* May 24, 1900, p. 2; May 31, pp. 1–2.

12. I take the conservative figures of Edgar Sydenstricker, "Collective Bargaining in the Anthracite Coal Industry," *Bulletin of the U.S. Bureau of Labor Statistics,* No. 191 (March, 1916), p. 18; Frank Julian Warne, "The Anthracite Coal Strike," *The Annals of the American Academy of Political and Social Science,* Vol. XVII (January, 1901), p. 15; John Mitchell, *Organized Labor* (Philadelphia, 1903), p. 366; Robert J. Cornell, *The Anthracite Coal Strike of 1902* (Published Ph.D. dissertation, Catholic University of America, 1957), p. 47; and *Reports of the Industrial Commission, Reports on Labor Organizations, Labor Disputes and Arbitration*

and on Railway Labor, Vol. XVII (Washington, D. C., 1900–1902), p. 191.

13. Fahy to Mitchell, September 18, 1900, in *John Mitchell Papers.*

14. As early as September 29 the Reading Railroad as shipper found the situation both "critical" and "desperate . . . owing to the stoppage of our anthracite mines." Letter-book, Philadelphia and Reading Railway Company, No. 1 Copying Book, September 27, 1900, p. 30, and September 29, p. 46, in Historical Society of Pennsylvania, Philadelphia. Peter Roberts, in *The Anthracite Coal Industry* (New York, 1901), pp. 186, 188, has the production losses: 4.5 million tons to 2.9 million tons, September 1899 and 1900; and 4.9 million to .8 million in October for both years.

15. Again this figure is conservative. District 9, for example, claimed three thousand members alone in December, 1900.

16. John Mitchell, "The Coal Strike," *McClure's Magazine,* Vol. XX (December, 1902), pp. 219–20.

17. Selig Perlman and Philip Taft, *History of Labor in the United States, 1896–1932: Labor Movements* (New York, 1935), Vol. IV, p. 36.

18. *Pottsville Republican,* October 19, 1900, p. 1; October 23, p. 1; October 24, p. 1; Mitchell to T. M. Davis, October 11, 1900, in *John Mitchell Papers.*

19. *Documents Relating to the Anthracite Coal Strike of 1902,* p. 95, in the U.S. Department of Labor Library, Washington, D. C.

20. *Ashland Advocate,* September 21, 1900, p. 2.

21. Fahy's observation to Mitchell, September 18, 1900, in *John Mitchell Papers,* validated in *Evening Herald,* September 19, 1900, p. 4.

22. *Public Ledger,* September 22, 1900, p. 16.

23. *Miners' Journal,* September 18, 1900, p. 1; September 19, p. 1; September 20, p. 1.

24. *Evening Herald,* September 14, 1900, p. 1.
25. *New York Herald,* September 23, 1900, p. 6.
26. *Plain Speaker,* September 23, 1900, p. 1.
27. *Chicago Times-Herald,* September 22, 1900, in *Markle Scrapbooks.*
28. *Chicago American,* September 22, 1900, in *Markle Scrapbooks.*
29. *New York Mail and Express,* September 29, 1900, in *Markle Scrapbooks.*
30. S. J. Kent to Mitchell, October 8, 1900, in *John Mitchell Papers.*
31. Earl W. Mayo, "On Strike!" *Frank Leslie's Popular Monthly,* Vol. LI (November, 1900), p. 45.
32. Of all the incidents noted I found only one in which Slavs acted more passively than the older nationalities. Immigrant participants in a march from McAdoo to Wilkes-Barre withdrew when Sheriff Harvey read them the riot act in Polish and English. *Rochester Herald,* September 26, 1900, and *Cleveland Plain Dealer,* September 26, 1900, in *Markle Scrapbooks.* Also there is a brief, unelaborated statement in "The Anthracite Coal Miners' Strike," *The Outlook,* Vol. LXVI (September 22, 1900), p. 187, which says: "The Hungarian, Italian and other immigrant miners have taken but little part in the strike, but the American miners have supported it almost uniformly."
33. Peter Roberts, *Anthracite Coal Industry* (New York, 1901), pp. 171–72.

CHAPTER IX: RESOLUTION, 1902

1. The union later reduced these to a 10-percent increase and a nine-hour day. Waldo E. Fisher, "Anthracite," in Labor Committee of the Twentieth Century Fund, *How Collective Bargaining Works* (New York, 1942), p. 290; Carroll Wright, "Report to the President on the Anthracite Coal Strike," *Bulletin of the Bureau of La-*

bor, No. 43 (November, 1902), pp. 1150–51; John Mitchell, *Organized Labor* (Philadelphia, 1903), p. 371.

2. Mitchell wanted the delay until "the late fall, when the men could have struck more effectively." Mitchell, *Organized Labor,* p. 373.

3. This tally is in Anthracite Coal Strike Commission, *Report to the President on the Anthracite Coal Strike of May-October, 1902* (Washington, D. C., 1903), p. 36, and elsewhere. Juveniles had fractional ballots.

4. Frank Norris, "Life in the Mining Region," *Everybody's Magazine,* VII (September, 1902), pp. 241–48. Some companies had erected real fortresses and even electrified the wires.

5. Once again the Lehigh independents demanded conditions from the men. Markle, Pardee, Coxe, and two others insisted that all returnees sign statements not to harm nonunion employees. When those strikers refused, as many as five thousand continued out some days longer. However, later most did sign the pledge.

6. *United Mine Workers' Journal,* November 15, 1900, p. 4.

7. Hammerling was a scoundrel, albeit a colorful one. Born in Galicia, he came to America about 1880, returned to Europe, then went to Hawaii, from where he reentered the United States illegally. He arrived in Wilkes-Barre and worked briefly as a mineworker. Later he acquired an interest in a Polish newspaper (probably Górnik) and solicited ads for the *United Mine Workers' Journal.* Through a shrewd business sense, a knowledge of foreign languages and a connection with Mitchell he grew wealthy in translating materials for the union and the Commonwealth of Pennsylvania. Always looking for a moneymaking opportunity, he capitalized on Mitchell's popularity in 1902, while at the same time he was suspected of working for the Lehigh and Wilkes-Barre Coal

Company. Later the rogue went to New York and illegally pressured the immigrant press first for the Republican party and later for the German cause in World War I. Deported for this, he married a Polish countess, became a Senator under Pilsudski, then returned to the United States, and during the Depression committed suicide by jumping out of a hotel window.

8. The Lehigh Valley station agents reported a "land office business" in such ticket sales. The *Daily Standard,* May 13, 1902, p. 1.

9. Charles B. Spahr, "The Miners' Strike: Impressions in the Field," *The Outlook,* Vol. LXXI (May 31, 1902), p. 323. Other destinations were neighboring farms and the mines of the far west.

10. Paul Ghio, "Histoire d'une Grève," *Journal des Économistes,* Vol. LIII (February 15, 1903), p. 183. See also *Scranton Times,* October 6, 1902, p. 5. Of course all these did not come from Slavic communities.

11. *Shenandoah Weekly Herald,* May 24, 1902, p. 1.

12. A definite union and immigrant cooperative movement did exist in the anthracite area. The paucity of records, however, hinders assessing its extent. Local 561 established its butchery in December, 1901. Its treasury dipped only from $200 in March, 1902, to $114 in late August, to the low point, $70, in mid-December. Even by July the group was contributing strike aid rather than requesting it. *Ksiazka Protokularna-Zjednoczonych Gorników w Ameryce Sekcya No. 561* (Springfield, Pennsylvania), pp. 46–47, 63, 85, 264–73.

13. And he concluded his report by listing huckleberry-picking and the outside employment of Slavic women and girls as effective aides. H. C. S., "Miners' Families Show No Signs of Poverty," *Public Ledger,* August 19, 1902, p. 3.

14. "Strike Good Thing for Green Ridge," *Plain Speaker*, September 14, 1902, p. 1.
15. One result was the secession of sixty-five Slovak and Polish mineworkers in Freeland from the Anglo-Saxon local to form their own Slavic affiliate, No. 309. Interview with its organizer, George Hudack, Mt. Pocono, Pa., June 2, 1962.
16. Pennsylvania Department of Internal Affairs, *Report of the Bureau of Mines . . . 1902* (Harrisburg, 1903), p. 34. The chart is taken from Edward Parker, "Coal," in U.S. Department of Commerce and Labor, U.S. Bureau of the Census, *Mines and Quarries, 1902* (Washington, D.C., 1905), p. 667.
17. *Plain Speaker,* May 15, 1902, p. 1. See also another statement of an East European leader in *ibid.,* May 16, p. 1.
18. *Ashland Advocate,* August 1, 1902, p. 3.
19. *Evening Herald,* August 7, 1902, p. 1.
20. As in 1900, the Polish religious leader, Father Lenarkiewicz, opposed the strike and warned his parishioners to beware of socialists.
21. *Telegraph* (Colorado Springs), July 31, 1902, in *John Mitchell Papers.*
22. *New York Herald,* August 6, 1902, p. 2.
23. *Daily News,* September 25, 1902, p. 1.
24. Interview with George Hudack, Mt. Pocono, Pa., June 2, 1962. He admitted that the groups rarely enforced the one-dollar fee, but it had a favorable psychological effect. Of course East Europeans alone did not persecute scabs and their families. Strikers generally organized lists and boycotts of merchants, landlords, and shopkeepers who traded with nonunion men. Even the taunts of breaker boys now going to school had an effect on the sons and daughters of scabs. Efforts by local police to combat this pressure were generally unsuccessful. The

Slavs, nevertheless, were particularly noteworthy in this situation. According to a Lithuanian his people won the special nickname of "Mustukas" (bullies) for their activity. But he added that Poles "also fought valiantly" in strikes. Frank Lavinskas and Antanas J. Banisauskas, *Miliukas's Epic and Sinful Deeds of Miserable Priests* (Long Island City, N. Y., 1952), p. 66.

25. *Straż,* May 17, 1902, p. 1; July 5, p. 3; July 26, p. 1. But the paper also warned against undue violence. August 16, p. 1.

26. One local announced its culprit: "Christ had a Judas; Caesar had a Brutus; . . . Washington had a Benedict Arnold; and the miners' union of No. 1 District has a Grimes." *United Mine Workers' Journal,* October 2, 1902, p. 7.

27. Walter Wellman quoted in Elsie Glück, *John Mitchell, Miner* (New York, 1929), p. 118.

28. Both quotes are in John Mitchell, "An Exposition and Interpretation of the Trade Union Movement," in Charles S. MacFarland, ed., *The Christian Ministry and the Social Order* (New Haven, 1913), pp. 95–96.

29. *New York Daily Tribune,* October 30, 1902, p. 14. The date is still a paid union holiday.

30. The third group, in addition to the union and the operators, consisted of the nonunion mineworkers who sought the same conditions as the UMW but whose counsel according to one report was in the pay of the coal companies. E. Dana Durand, "The Anthracite Coal Strike," *Political Science Quarterly,* Vol. XVIII (September, 1903), pp. 388–89.

31. Anthracite Coal Strike Commission, 1902–1903, *Proceedings of the Anthracite Coal Strike Commission* (56 vols., Washington, D. C., 1903), Vol. LVI, pp. 9990, 9992, 9995, 10021.

CHAPTER X: CONCLUSION

1. House of Representatives, 57th Congress, 1st Session, Document No. 184, *Reports of the Industrial Commission, Reports on Immigration, Including Testimony, with Review and Digest and Special Reports* (Washington, D. C., 1901), Vol. XV, p. 312.

2. *Reports of the Industrial Commission, Reports on Labor Organizations, Labor Disputes and Arbitration and on Railway Labor* (Washington, D. C., 1900–1902), Vol. XVII, p. 184.

3. Grover G. Huebner, "The Americanization of the Immigrant," *The Annals of the American Academy of Political and Social Science,* Vol. XXVIII (May, 1906), p. 206; and William Z. Ripley, "Race Factors in Labor Unions," *The Atlantic Monthly,* Vol. XCIII (March, 1904), p. 301. Just a year after the famous hard-coal dispute, Edward Kirk Titus, in "The Pole in the Land of the Puritan," *New England Magazine,* Vol. XXIV (October, 1903), p. 164, noted that Poles never strike!

4. G. M. Stevenson, "Immigrant Labor," in James Truslow Adams and R. V. Coleman, eds., *Dictionary of American History* (New York, 1940), Vol. III, pp. 72–73.

5. David Brody, *Steelworkers in America: The Non-Union Era* (Cambridge, Mass., 1960), pp. 100–103, 106, 108, 136, 246.

6. *Ibid.,* p. 139.

7. Admittedly some "immigrants" were strikebreakers. However, it was probably the union policy of excluding the unskilled which caused its failure in steel. Leon Wolff, *Lockout: The Story of the Homestead Strike of 1892* (New York, 1965), pp. 17–18, 111, 128–29, 169, 229, and a review by W. V. Wallace in the *Journal of American Studies,* Vol. I (April, 1967), pp. 134–35.

8. The general instability and disorganization, then, de-

scribed in Rowland Berthoff, "The Social Order of the Anthracite Region, 1825–1902," *Pennsylvania Magazine of History and Biography,* Vol. LXXXIX (July, 1965), especially pp. 286–291, did not seem to exist in the East European case.

9. A recent historian has described briefly the nationalities' reaction at Lawrence in 1913: "By the end of January the strike was clearly a revolt of the newer immigrants led by radicals and supported with comparatively little enthusiasm by English speaking operatives," and he concluded on the effect and extent of the immigrant response: "Perhaps the tactics of the strikers frightened the more established nationalities. Women, many of them wives of the strikers, trod the frozen streets beside their men and occupied the front ranks in demonstrations and parades." Edwin Fenton, "Immigrants and Unions, a Case Study: Italians and American Labor, 1870–1920" (Unpublished Ph.D. dissertation, Harvard University, 1957), pp. 338–39; and see also pp. 354–55, 371–72. Note similarities in John Ingham, "A Strike in the Progressive Era; McKees Rocks, 1909," *Pennsylvania Magazine of History and Biography,* Vol. XC (July, 1966), pp. 359 ff.

10. My italics. Peter Roberts, *Anthracite Coal Communities* (New York, 1904), p. 36.

11. William M. Leiserson, *Adjusting Immigrant and Industry* (New York, 1924), p. 227.

12. Jack Barbash, "Ethnic Factors in the Development of the American Labor Movement," *Industrial Relations Research Association* (December, 1952), p. 82.

Index

257

Roosevelt, Theodore, 180–181, 199, 200
Russia, 14–17, 21–23, 26–27, 31
Ryscavage (Ryskiewicz), Adam, 183, 199

saloons, 47–49, 52, 57, 113–114
Schlosser, Anthony, 183, 189–190, 195, 198, 199, 202
Schuylkill field:
  and WBA, 62–63, 64, 65, 66–67
  East European arrival in, 35–37, 69
  in strikes, 66–68, 72–75, 87, 89, 91, 144–145, 165–170, 187, 196
  location and description, 5–6
  resistance to unionization, 112–113
  UMW organization in, 122, 158–159, 160, 161
Scranton, 3, 4, 38, 71–74, 81, 141, 164
Septek, "Big Mary," 143–144
Shamokin, 4, 5, 35, 66, 69, 70, 75, 87, 88, 122, 125, 141, 164, 165, 179, 183
Shenandoah, 4, 5, 35–37, 48, 55, 56, 69, 70, 75, 94, 100–108, 109, 119, 125, 141, 164, 166–170, 173, 175, 184, 187, 190–194, 196
Shenandoah City mine, 101, 167, 191
Sheppton, 4, 5, 39, 170–173
Siney, John, 62, 82, 86–87
Slavic children:
  as mineworkers, 49–52

economic role, 44–45, 186
in strikes, 143, 186
Slavic women:
  function of, in household, 44–45, 185
  in strikes, 101, 143–144, 157, 171, 172, 175, 195
Slavs:
  as strikebreakers, 80, 114
  as strikers, 157–158, 160, 169, 174–175, 184–203, 205–206, 209–213
  enter anthracite fields, 60–61, 113
  in 1887–1888 strike, 95
  in 1897 strike, 130–132, 139, 141–142, 143–144, 147–151
  in 1900 strike, 165, 166–167, 168, 169–170
  in 1902 strike, 177, 186–190, 194, 195–203, 205–206
  organizability, 153–158, 182–183
  savings, 54–58, 118–120, 173–174, 184–188
  temperance and, 113–114
  wages, 52–53
  work performance as mineworkers, 49, 114, 129–130, 157
Slovaks:
  in Lattimer Massacre, 138, 140, 147
  in strikes, 107, 128, 130, 166, 171, 197
  in Pennsylvania, 35 ff., 100
  real estate purchases of, 120
  wealth of, in Hazleton, 55
Southern field. See Schuylkill field